# FEAR GOD, NOT EVIL

## FASCINATING UNFORGETTABLE TRUE STORIES

### JODIE RANDISI

ISBN 978-0-9960533-1-0 (eBook edition)

ISBN 978-0-9960533–3-4 (Print edition)

*This book is dedicated to my sweetheart, Joe Randisi, whose faithfulness in answering God's call for his life has moved and inspired me to start and finish many projects, especially this book, and whose perseverance and pursuit of excellence has ministered to so many, some happen to be in Christian ministry. My husband is my personal hero because without his support and steadfast faith in me as a writer, I would not have attempted such a project. However, God gets the glory. Joe, on the other hand, gets my love, admiration, and respect.*

*May we shine brightly, live greatly, and remember all the Holy Spirit has taught us.*

# CONTENTS

# PREFACE

I've been reading *Streams in the Desert,* a Christian daily devotional written by Mrs. Charles Cowman, since 2008. I found the book in the free pile at the Hilton Head Library. Mrs. Cowman's devotional has been considered a classic since it was first published in 1925. The title comes from the scripture verse found in the book of Isaiah 43, verse 19—*I am making a way in the desert and streams in the wasteland.*

According to the inscription I found on the title page, this particular book was originally given to (and perhaps left by) *Ken and Ginny* from *Tim and Sally* in 1982. I've been highlighting and dating passages, recording names, and making comments in the margins ever since stumbling upon this treasure. Due to its constant use, I had to reconstitute the book by extracting its pages from the original binding and preserving them in an odd-sized, binder.

Over the decades, this devotional has nourished my walk with Christ. I often thought, how did Mrs. Cowman know I needed these exact words on this particular day to rejuvenate my spirit?

Of course, I realize the Holy Spirit is the source, and so I give thanks and all the glory goes to God.

I found the following passage of great interest because it accurately describes my baptism of the Holy Spirit experience, after which I became evangelical.

> *But you will receive power when the Holy Spirit comes on you; and you will be my witnesses in Jerusalem, and in all Judea and Samaria, and to the ends of the earth.* Acts 1:8

My efforts to witness the love of Jesus was not always welcomed. Some friends and family members would say I went to the extreme. My zeal at the time was not gifted, or proficient. Oh well.

Here's the passage that brings to remembrance my baptism of the Holy Spirit followed by the reason it is included here.

DECEMBER 17

"All at once, I felt as though a hand—not feeble, but omnipotent; not of wrath, but of love— was laid on my brow (in my case, belly). I felt it not outwardly but inwardly. It seemed to press upon my whole being, and to diffuse all through me a holy, sin-consuming energy. As it passed downward, my heart as well as my head was conscious of the presence of this soul-cleansing energy, under the influence (in my case, like ripples of the lake's surface after a pebble has been tossed in from above) of which I fell on the floor (in my case, woke up) and in the joyful surprise of the moment, cried out in a loud voice. For a few minutes the deep ocean of God's love (filled me); all its waves and billows rolled over me."

That was the testimony of Bishop Hamline.

When my husband and I became good friends with the gifted and highly effective evangelist, Denny Nissley, I was fascinated by his stories. Church people who heard him preach continually asked Denny, "Where can I get your book?" He'd reply, "I'm too busy living to stop and write a book." BINGO! This is when I realized I could be his scribe, and together we penned *Fear NO Evil, The Story of Denny Nissley and Christ in Action*.

*Fear No Evil* was my first attempt at writing book. I'm an educator by trade and degree, not an English or journalism major. However, the book was published in 1999 because I paid $75 for a manuscript review and Denny had just been arrested for carrying a ten-foot wooden cross in a Christmas parade. To our delight, our book proposal was selected. However, it was the last book chosen for publication before Waterbrook, a division of Random House, purchased Harold Shaw Publishing. It was quite a thrill to have my first book traditionally published.

Now that two decades have passed since *Fear NO Evil* was published, I've come to the realization that the content could use some rejuvenation, primarily because there is no eBook version available. Also, I'm a more experienced writer and publisher. From my perspective, the original manuscript was not adequately edited. Perhaps the original publisher was under the gun to get it out before new publishing house took over. In any case, I was left with misgivings about this version of the book because I knew it could be better. For example, the last chapter was removed and replaced without my knowledge. It came as a surprise when I received the galley copy in the mail.

"It's his story. He gets the final say."

That was understandable, except I had in mind what I call a circle close. The last chapter was intended to tie a ribbon around the concept that Christians should not fear evil when following God's calling for their lives. Instead, a chapter on the ministry's disaster relief efforts had replaced the amazing final story I had submitted, which undeniably validated the premise of *Fear NO Evil*.

I was disappointed but also dismayed that I was not informed of the decision to change the book's conclusion. Christ in Action's disaster relief ministry efforts could be (and should be) another entire book; that's how I interpreted the situation. I harbor no ill will, but it is what propelled me to master the craft and business of self-publishing by establishing my publishing company, COWCATCHER Publications, and the writing of this book, *Fear GOD, Not Evil.*

# INTRODUCTION

Hitmen services are available in many nations across the world, but would it surprise you to learn that, in this case, in order to get a hitman assigned to you, all you'd have to do is preach the gospel on the streets of America?

Denny was a miserable excuse for a human being before his conversion to Christianity. Despite being raised in a churchgoing family, Denny found himself on a path of self-destruction in the '70s—a drug addict and alcoholic leading a life of crime. I found his reversal-of-destiny story remarkable and worth sharing, which is why I coauthored his book, *Fear NO Evil - The Story of Denny Nissley and Christ in Action* in 1999.

Denny's dramatic testimony has affected thousands of people, many thousands, actually. His deep devotion to sharing Christ where it's *"most desperately needed and hardest to find"* is unconventional, engaging, and empowering. His passion is contagious and the reason I decided to republish his amazing true stories. Denny is a masterful storyteller. His stories are riveting and best told by him. You'll find them described this way: *In his own words...*

Before his conversion in April of 1977, Denny was an incorrigible, shameless, callous criminal. His incredible transformation from a drug and alcohol addicted holy terror into a wholly devoted man of God is truly miraculous. He is a devoted husband to his wife Sandy, the father of their eleven children, and grandfather to, well, the count is ongoing, so let's just say, if it already isn't dozens, it will be eventually. The man does not have time to write books. That's where I come in.

Denny, like magician Penn Jillette, disagrees with those who say faith is a private matter. Penn Jillette is the verbal half of the magician duo Penn and Teller and known to be an outspoken atheist. Jillette has stated he doesn't respect people who don't proselytize. Jillette asks, "How much do you have to hate someone to not proselytize? How much do you have to hate somebody to believe that everlasting life is possible and not tell them that?"

For Denny, attracting people to Christ is a public matter, perhaps because he's notably qualified to reach unlikely candidates for conversion, the people who would never darken the doorway of a church. Over the decades, Denny has ministered to prostitutes, pimps, professional hitmen, gang members, drug addicts, alcoholics, as well as businessmen, diplomats, and politicians. He has been shot at, threatened with knives, beaten unconscious, and put in jail for preaching the gospel. His skillful effort to pioneer churches brought him national recognition in 1991 when he was awarded an honorary Doctorate of Evangelism from Columbia Evangelical Seminary in Longview, Washington.

As a minister of the gospel, Denny will do whatever it takes to win the lost, including feeding entire neighborhoods. His practically fool-proof philosophy has worked for decades, and that is—it's hard for unbelievers to speak unfavorably about Christians when their bellies are full of free food.

The stories in this book are true and verified. I've always been attracted to stories that clearly demonstrate God's affinity for using ordinary people to accomplish extraordinary things. As a friend and long-time supporter of Christ in Action ministries, I've been exposed to their amazing true stories for years. Each dramatic anecdote unveils Denny's "Holy Ghost hutzpah," which I'm confident will ignite a desire to be an effective and bold witness for Christ, that is, if you're a believer. If you're reading this, and you haven't taken a step of faith towards believing in God's plan for recovery from sin, my hope and prayer is that you will trust in the Lord and invite Him to rescue you from eternal separation from God.

For the believer and disciple of Christ, these chapters will prove to be a provocative read, sure to challenge the stagnate state of affairs in our attempts to share the love of God and his plan for salvation. If, after reading these stories, you, like me, are pricked in your heart to become a bolder and more effective witness for Jesus, I invite you to take advantage of the bonus offer found at the end of this book.

Exposure to one minister's experiences and belief that the power of God is readily available to those who dare to put their trust in Him should convince believers in Christ that we can rest assured —greater is He who is us than he who is in the world. In other words, there's no reason to fear evil.

# OBSESSED WITH CHAOS

Denny Nissley is a master storyteller with an abundance of marvelous stories to relate, but he repeats one story more than all the others, and that is his testimony of how he became a Christian. Although he was raised in a loving Christian home, he was determined not to be like those "Jesus freaks," a phrase he used to refer to anyone who had the gall to talk about Jesus as if he were real.

The stark contrast of Denny's wild rebellious days to his outcome as the founder and director of Christ in Action ministries (CIA) clearly demonstrates God's interest in redeeming derelicts. Denny has given his testimony on radio and television talk shows, has been featured on the 700 Club and the Canadian television program 100 Huntley Street. When he speaks to church congregations and Christian organizations, audiences are enthralled by his outrageous stories. The best place to begin is the beginning.

*In his own words...*

The first time I got drunk I was thirteen. My buddies and I camped out at the edge of the Susquehanna River so that when five o'clock in the morning came, we could have our hooks in the water for the first moments of trout season. Someone brought six bottles of Boone's Farm apple wine, and as a result, I never saw a fish or laid hands on a fishing rod.

The wine tasted so sweet. Even after consuming an entire bottle, it didn't seem to bother me...until I stood up. Then it hit me like a ton of bricks. The world spun out of control. Trees began to multiply. As I tried to decide which one to grab onto for support, I lost control. While throwing up, I thought, *I'm miserable. Why would anyone like getting drunk? I'll never do this again!"*

But deep down inside I knew I would do it again, even though the next morning my head throbbed, my stomach ached, and it felt as if an army of ants in muddy boots had camped out in my mouth. Unfortunately, my friends at school made the mistake of asking me, "Hey, Denny, what'd you do this weekend?"

So, I told them. "A bunch of us partied down by the river and I got stinking' drunk. I was smashed out of my mind," I bragged.

"Really? Wow, that's cool."

Instantly, I had a reputation to live up to. I felt obligated to go when invited to weekend beer parties. By the time I was sixteen, I was drinking and doing drugs constantly. Getting stoned on weed at school was my normal routine, but because I was a member of the wrestling team, I keep myself from going wild during the week. Besides, alcohol, not drugs, was the object of my heart's desire.

Over the years, I progressed from being a drug and alcohol user to a hard-core drug and alcohol abuser. I successfully burnt my memory with marijuana, fried my mind with LSD, and then scorched my brain with speed. I washed it all down with my favorite companion, a can of Budweiser, the king of beers.

The staff at Solanco High School decided to quietly adjust the curve in their grading system so they wouldn't have to deal with my obnoxious mouth and corrupt behavior any longer than necessary. They wanted me gone. Six days before graduation, the principal called me into his office.

"Mr. Nissley," the principal addressed me, "I called you in here to tell you that you're not graduating because you made the grades. You're moving on because we don't want you back here next year."

After barely graduated from high school, I went to work as a welder. One by one, I traded in my old friends for new drinking buddies. I needed at least three cases of beer a week to be able to function enough to keep my job. On top of that, I needed several additional cases to keep my friends supplied. I supplemented my income with midnight burglaries of country stories and gas stations. The liquid courage I found in a can caused me to do things I would never have done if I had been in my right mind.

Each time I sobered up, these vicious things haunted me. The only solution I could think of was to stay drunk, so that's what I did. I went to work drunk, and came home to get drunk. My life was one prolonged blurry preoccupation with drunken orgies, bar brawls, and criminal activities. My friends nickname me "The Funnel."

Needless to say, I was a huge disappointment to my Christian parents. I had no intention of becoming such a pain in the neck for my mom and dad. I didn't have a good reason to rebel. I attended Sunday school, learned the expected set of Bible verses, and went to church with my dad, mom, brother, and sister. My happy childhood was spent exploring the simple pleasures of good country living, that is until I decided to follow my friends and not my Christian upbringing. Any godly seeds sown in my heart as a young boy were gobbled up by my decision to allow sin to take over my life.

## SOMETHING'S NOT RIGHT AND IT HURTS!

With disdain, I ignored the warning and admonitions of friends and relatives about the consequence of my riotous lifestyle. Then, one day at work, I had a crisis. Without warning, twelve hundred pounds of compressed cardboard fell on me. The material came down like a wall and buried me, pinning me to the warehouse floor. As I dug my way out, I noticed my left foot at my waist, and if that wasn't bad enough, I was pretty sure it was bent the wrong way. I looked at the backside of my knee and thought, *This isn't right, and it hurts! Something is very wrong here. I have a feeling I'm in big trouble.*

In a panic, I grabbed my foot and tried to throw back into place, thinking it might somehow pop back in place. It didn't. My coworkers rushed me to the hospital where the doctors took x-rays and followed up with tests while my lifeless leg hung limp in an air splint.

"You know, Mr. Nissley, you're young. You're agile. It shouldn't be too hard to learn how to walk with a prosthetic leg."

The doctor's prognosis was amputation two inches above the knee. My violent temper filled the room. I grabbed a crutch and tried my best to beat the doctor. As I was reaching and swinging, the doctor crawled under the bed and escaped out the door. I managed grab a handful of syringes and flung them at the fleeing physician. He decided it might be in everyone's best interest if I got a second opinion.

"I hear you're opposed to amputation," a different doctor stated. "There is something else we might try."

I would have to endure a total of nine operations and commit to extensive physical therapy. It was the only alternative to amputation. Surgeries included transplanting muscles while removing ligaments and cartilage. Orthopedic surgeons retracted my kneecap and reattached muscles to bones with stainless steel staples. A customized braced helped me walk. They told me it would work for five to seven years, but then the leg would have to come off. There was no way to make it last longer, let alone permanently. However, there were some benefits.

## FOLLOWING DOCTOR'S ORDERS

I pushed the call button for the nurse to bring in another bottle of my favorite beer and thought, *This is room service at its finest.* Despite being seriously injured and in a hospital, life was relatively good.

The doctors agreed that I was a special case, in that sudden detoxification from alcohol would cause me more harm than good. They thought they were being both practical and merciful when they prescribed a realist dosage of alcohol—a least a six-pack of per day—as a way to make my stay less traumatic. But their primary concern was to avoid the grisly symptoms of alcoholic withdrawal known as the DTs. The doctors' worst fear was that leg spasms would rip apart crucial stitches and the staples embedded within my severely damaged leg.

My buddies and I devised ways to make life even better. We combined forces and supplemented my prescription with whiskey smuggled in under their jackets and get well wishes. After a couple of drunken weeks, I finally left the hospital, though I returned from time to time for the other eight surgeries.

Between trips to the hospital, I spent a year and a half on crutches and in physical therapy. The only thing I knew to do was to drink a case of beer and half a fifth of tequila every day while collecting Workman's Compensation and Social Security checks. These were the benefits of being labeled permanently disabled, or so I thought.

Then someone told my parents, who had been patiently loving me through all of this, that I was abusing heavy drugs, not just alcohol. After two years of waiting on me hand and foot, my parents confronted me, hoping I would come to my senses. It didn't work. They decided to evict their slug of a son.

I thought I had figured out who ratted me out and decided he deserved a good beating, but when I found him, instead of fighting, we talked. Charlie listened as I griped about my pending eviction.

"Just go to church," he told me.

"No way! I'd rather die!" I responded.

But after giving it some thought, I decided if I went, at least my parents would get off my back for a while and I could continue my rent-free living arrangement. Plus, I would have enough funds to support my growing addictions and obsession with chaos.

# MEDICAL MIRACLE

When sinners go to church they often feel like long-tailed cats in a room full of rocking chairs. This was especially true for wild man Denny Nissley, the guy who had most likely committed every sin ever invented. Nevertheless, he took a chance and went to a church in southern Lancaster County, Pennsylvania. This church facility was a big barn, which made it seemed less dangerous than a traditional church.

The Jesus freaks immediately got on his nerves. After that first visit, he couldn't stop thinking about what they had going on that made them so happy. To the delight and satisfaction of his parents, they convinced him to go back a second time.

On that morning, Denny sat by the back door with his friend Charlie. The preacher did his number and the salvation invitation began. Denny had heard it all many times before. "With every head bowed, every eye closed..."

*In his own words...*

I was thinking about what I'd be doing right after the service ended. I could almost taste the beer going down my funnel. Then something captured my attention.

"Someone in here doesn't believe Jesus is real," the preacher stated.

I said to myself, *Yeah, you got that right. It's me. How does he know what I'm thinking?*

"If you don't believe Jesus is real, then why don't you put Him to the test? If you ask Him, He will make Himself real to you."

*Okay, God. If you're up there, and I really don't think you are, I want you to let me know.* That was my prayer.

All six feet, one inch, two hundred pounds of me slowly drifted to the left, toward Charlie. I opened my eyes to see if I was crowding my friend, but Charlie wasn't there. I looked around. It wasn't Charlie who had moved; I had.

I was standing halfway up the aisle, headed to the front of the barn. This, in itself, was a miracle since I never intended to respond to anything during a church service. I was convinced churches were for weaklings and hypocrites.

I was a maximum tough guy, a bouncer at some of the county's rowdiest bars. I obtained this employment by thrashing the existing bouncer and throwing him out the door, after which, I found the manager to ask for his job. Tough guys full of themselves don't go to church, let alone respond to an altar call.

Another thing dumbfounded me. In addition to not being able to recall walking down the aisle, the usual throbbing in my leg was absent. In fact, my leg didn't hurt at all. I looked around. It seemed as if everyone was looking at me. Others were going forward, so I followed them. They knelt down, which was a problem for me since I had only one good knee, but somehow, I got down on my knees, too.

The moment I knelt down, I began to weep. A stockpile of shame surfaced, then something supernatural happened. I let go of years of mental and emotional anguish that had been covered up and numbed by my devotion to substance abuse. I couldn't explain or stop the unrestrained tears. I sobbed like a baby.

The preacher came over and asked, "What do you want?"

"I don't know. I don't know what I want."

"Do you want Jesus?"

"Yeah, I guess so," I said.

The preacher and another man grabbed my hands and prayed. In a circle of three, I received Jesus, my Savior. Tears of shame and remorse were instantaneously driven out by an incredible inner peace.

"I have to sit down," I told them. "I've got a bum knee."

They probably thought I had a knee injury from playing football, perhaps a strain or something of that nature.

"Jesus will heal that leg just as He did when He walked on the earth," they informed me. "Would you like us to pray for you?"

"Yeah, sure, go for it." I figured I'd try anything once.

They finished praying and announced, "You're healed."

"Really?"

"Sure! Go ahead and walk. Stand up and try it out. See for yourself."

And I did. I was totally pain free for the first time in two years.

"WOW!" I cried out loud. *Maybe God healed my leg!*

I rolled up my pant leg and took off the brace. It was then that they knew this was not just an 'owie.' They couldn't help noticing the enormous scars that ran up and down my leg. All of a sudden, they realized they had prayed for a bona fide cripple.

I started to walk and the leg stayed in the right place, precisely where it was supposed to be. Like an escaped maniac, I freaked out. I ran around the barn, jumping over benches in a state of extreme exhilaration.

"Man! What are you all looking at?" I shouted at the congregation. "God just healed my blankety-blank leg!"

No one reprimanded me for swearing in church. Instead, shouts of joy went up before the Lord. "Praise God! Hallelujah!"

I realized I had finally reached true freedom and that God was real. My notion of a longhaired guru sitting on the top of a mountain holding a big stick ready to clobber sinners was gone. God was not some pie in the sky or special occasion cake. I finally understood that He is the Bread of Life made for everyday use.

Miracle upon miracle, the day I became a born-again believer was the same day I was delivered of drug and alcohol addiction. On the way home, I pulled out my cigarettes, put one in my mouth, pushed in the lighter, and thought, *This feels funny here in my mouth. I don't need this anymore!*

I crumpled up the pack of cigarettes and started to throw them out the car window. Then I had a strange thought. *Wait a minute. That wouldn't be right. That's God's country. I'd be littering.* I threw the trash on the floor instead. With refreshing clarity, I noticed how everything had changed.

It became overwhelmingly obvious to everyone who knew Denny that all his ungodly, angry, bitter, racist, perverted thoughts were gone. He had a new mysterious affection for people. New habits replaced unhealthy ones. His mother, Betty, and his father, Ernie, couldn't have been happier. They could not wait to tell Denny's aunts and uncles and all the folks at church who had been praying for his salvation what had happened. They wanted everyone to know that Denny Nissley had not only received Christ, but God healed his severely damaged leg and delivered him from all his addictions—all at once!

It was the great news everyone needed and wanted to hear. It happened on April 3, 1977, the most glorious day of Denny Nissley's life.

## VERIFIED AND UNDENIABLE

Shortly after Denny's conversion, the doctors at Temple University Hospital scheduled an extensive battery of tests that would take nearly eight hours to complete. To their amazement, they discovered the ligaments and cartilage they had removed had grown back. Transplanted muscles had returned to their normal locations, and the stainless-steel staples they had drilled into his bones had vanished. The evidence couldn't have been clearer. On the Friday before the church service, Denny measured 15% strength in his bum leg. On Monday after the service, he measured 97% strength in his healed leg. Documented by medical professionals, Denny Nissley's healing was, and is, an indisputable medical miracle.

He found out later that his physical therapist was profoundly affected by what had happened to Denny and his leg. He told God that he was going to watch Denny for thirty days, and if they dramatic changes proved to be permanent, then he, too, would serve God. Apparently, God had to prove to this man that He could heal a shattered life as well as a shattered leg.

Denny used to think God turned people into freaks. The truth is quite the opposite. God's love transforms people into fulfilled and productive humans, and nobody is beyond His reach. Denny is a prime example of God's unconditional love. God spared Denny's life when He saved Solanco High class of 1973's "most likely to die of an overdose."

God filled Denny's funnel with streams of living water and called him into full-time ministry. A thousand cases of beers never satisfied Denny's thirst, but one taste of Jesus' prescription of Living Water gave my friend what he needed and much more than he could have imagined was even possible. And it came with a lifetime guarantee—a lifetime filled with incredible hope, extraordinary love, innumerable blessings, unparalleled peace, tremendous joy, remarkable miracles, and a retirement plan good enough to die for.

# BIBLE SCHOOL REBELS

enny hadn't given marriage any thought until he met Sandy James, a student from Christ for the Nations Bible School. In 1981, Denny was a 26-year-old, fiery street preacher and the self-appointed president of the *Bachelor til the Rapture* club. He had dedicated himself to doing as much damage as he could in the devil's own territory on the streets of America. Denny was sure God hadn't made a woman who could tie him down. The amazing part is not that he gave up bachelorhood. The most amazing part is that he proposed on their second date, and he and Sandy were married after being in each other's presence only six times.

Here's how it happened. Denny met Sandy in New Orleans on an outreach being held during Mardi Gras. He realized who she was in Lancaster, Pennsylvania. They had their first date in Washington, D.C. He proposed in Illinois and Sandy received her engagement ring in Cleveland, Ohio. To celebrate, they had receptions in Ohio, Pennsylvania, Oklahoma, and Colorado. In Frog Hollow, Virginia, they found out they were expecting their first child. Rachel Nissley was born in Greeley, Colorado. All of that took place within a span of eighteen months. This prolific pace is representative of Denny and Sandy's drive and passion for living a fully devoted life dedicated to the glory of God.

There is no doubt that God handpicked Denny and Sandy to be a unified couple in their pursuit of family and ministry. Since the beginning, the Nissleys have continually experienced God's goodness and supernatural blessing. Every year, on September 12th, they celebrate the day the president of the *Bachelor til the Rapture* club listened to the Holy Ghost, gave up the post, and tied the knot.

Denny has had numerous death threats because of his outspoken faith in Christ. They began in Dallas, Texas, where he attended Christ for the Nations Institute. The man never excelled academically, but it wasn't because of his lack of a proper high school education. It was because of his overwhelming desire to minister to the pimps and prostitutes while attending Bible School. He found himself more interested in what was happening on the streets of downtown Dallas than what was taking place in the classroom. On the streets, he was exceedingly successful.

God called Denny to Bible school a year and a half after being born again. When he told his friends, they questioned him. "Are you sure, Denny? You can't even spell Bible school." Although that might have been an exaggeration, it was true that he never studied a day in his godless life. He couldn't remember completing one homework assignment. The only reason he carried a book around in school was in case someone messed with him. He used books to defend himself and to attack any poor soul who was stupid enough to challenge the big guy.

*In his own words...*

14

Going to Bible school seemed absurd, but I knew it was God's plan for my life. When someone mentioned Christ for the Nations, I decided to go there. I sent a letter, bought a three-piece suit, cut my hair, and moved to Dallas. While a student there, I took small teams of zealous students to downtown for street ministry excursions. In my heart, I knew God wanted me to reach out to the prostitutes on Cedar Springs Avenue, a notorious strip for picking up ladies of the night. I also felt a burden to reach out to the pimps. Unfortunately, pimps, hookers, and Bible school students don't keep the same hours, so I had to break a few rules to save a few souls.

I'll be the first to confess my burden for street people affected my better judgement. I frequently stayed out past the 11 PM curfew on weekends to minister to the perverts, pimps, prostitutes, and anyone else within earshot.

## BE STILL AND KNOW

One of Denny's street ministry partners was a New Yorker, a Puerto Rican named Evelyn. She stood all of four feet, eleven inches tall. While she was a hooker, Evelyn had been saved and discipled at the New Life for Girls program. She proved to be the perfect partner for one particular street ministry excursion.

It was way past curfew when Evelyn and Denny came face to face with a disgruntled pimp on a sidewalk.

**In his own words...**

"I don't like you being here," the pimp said. "How 'bout I take your woman here and put her into some white slavery?"

"Over my dead body," I said courageously.

The next thing I knew a long, cold blade rested on my Adam's apple. I didn't know where it came from or how it got there, but when the cutting edge began to gently press down on my flesh, I stopped wondering and stood still.

The pimp looked at me with eyes of steel and said, "That can be arranged."

I believed him. It occurred to me that my Bible school teachers had not yet covered what to do when an angry pimp puts a knife to your throat. *Was it possible I missed that class?*

I stood there while intense fear began to invade my thoughts. *Where did the man with the faith and power for the hour go? It's ain't me, God. I'm scared! I'm gonna die, and I'm thinking I don't want to die right now.*

Mr. How 'Bout I Take Your Woman decided to press a little harder until a trickle of warm blood ran down my neck. I didn't even have to look. I knew that if I sneezed, my Adam's apple was going to get cored. *Be still and know that I am God.* That was the only scripture that came to mind.

So, I stood there, paralyzed. I thought, *Oh, God, what am I going to do? Lord, this would be a good time for a lightning strike. Why don't you just smite this pest with a bolt?*

Actually, in a very short period of time, I compiled a list of twenty different ways God could eradicate this heartless reprobate. Then, suddenly, out of the blue, Evelyn with arms flailing, exploded like a bottle rocket.

"Man! You don't know what chou're doing! Don't chou know who this is, man? This man is God's holy property, man! And chou got a knife stuck on his throat? Don't chou know what God could do to you, man?"

I thought, *Woman! You don't know what you're doing! Chou gonna get me kilt. Please be quiet.*

I never heard a Puerto Rican ex-hooker rant and rave so fast, so hard, so long, and so harsh in all my life. I thought, *this isn't the plan I had in mind, but I guess I don't have a say in it because I'm busy being still—knowing God.*

She finally shut up, but she wasn't finished. She glared at him with her cockiest look, eyes wide open, eyebrows raised up to her hairline, hands on her hips, and her ninety-nine-pound body poised like a deadly weapon.

The pimp looked at her. Then he looked at me and pulled the knife away from my throat, folded it back up, put it in his pocket, and ran away like a scared rabbit.

"Evelyn! You almost got me killed!"

"Chut up, man. Chou're bleedin'."

The ministry team of New York Evelyn and Denny Nissley decided at this point the outreach was over. After we thanked God for sparing our lives, I dropped Evelyn off at her dormitory and drove around Dallas in my pickup truck, reflecting on the night's events. Later that night, my roommate, another godly man named Charlie, showed up at just the right time. Charlie helped me slip into the dorm unnoticed.

Charlie didn't go on the covert outreaches. He stayed up late so he could let me in after hours. When Charlie looked at me, he felt sorry for the sinners who had to spend another night on the streets with the extreme evangelist. When I looked at Charlie, I saw a pastor in the making. I'd be the one to drag them in; he'd be the one to teach them apologetics, or whatever else I was supposed to be learning at Bible school.

Charlie and I were perfect counterparts. Before coming to Christ for the Nations, Charlie had study habits. I had drug and alcohol habits. Years later, it occurred to me, Charlie Barton and I were ideal teammates. It was the Lord who put us together so we could make a difference in nabbing souls for the kingdom of God.

## WRESTLING WITH GOD

As I lay in bed, thinking about what had just taken place that night, I thanked God again for getting rid of the angry pimp. Then I asked the Lord the precarious question, *God, why didn't you just take him out?*

"Denny, you really don't believe in me."

*What?*

"You really don't believe in me, not really."

*God, I sure do believe in you. Remember me? I gave up drugs and alcohol for you. I'm going to Bible school. I cut my hair for you. I'm preaching your gospel! What do you mean, I don't believe in you?*

Like a tape recorder in my mind, God took me through the evening's events. All at once, I realized my thoughts and desires for the knife-wielding pimp did not line up with God's thoughtsZZZZ and desires. I wanted God to destroy him, and God wanted to save him from an eternity in hell.

"You wished he would die on Cedar Springs Avenue and go to hell because you don't believe in me. You love your life more than you love me. You don't believe enough in me to say, Lord, it's okay with me if you take me out of this world."

After wrestling with God for an hour, I felt I had to go over this with Charlie.

"Charlie, wake up! I don't even believe in God, man!"

"Yes, you do, Denny. You're a Christian."

"No, I don't. You're not going to believe what happened tonight."

I tried to explain the impasse. The two of us knelt by the side of my bed. We prayed for a good while, then Charlie went back to bed. The first glimpse of morning light found me still seeking God. During the hours of complete honesty in which I emptied myself before God, I surrendered my life, never to take it back again. God wanted me to trust Him exclusively.

I let God search my heart and expose the thoughts and attitudes He knew what was holding me back from pursuing His will wholeheartedly. I gave up control of every aspect of my life, especially my ministry. I cried out to God to forgive my selfish attitudes. I lamented over my lack of compassion. I begged for cleansing from my Heavenly Father.

From that day forward, I knew God would work through me without being hampered by my selfish desire to live. I had acquired an undeniable, reverential longing to be with God. I was living without the fear of death, but that's not to say I didn't have opportunities to be fearful. In fact, I had several more opportunities to imagine my home-going while I was still a student who, between late night trips to Cedar Springs Avenue, sometimes studied the Bible.

# I'M GONNA KILL YOU

Denny came up with a brilliant plan to rescue a prostitute from her deplorable life on the streets. Shirley had given her life to the Lord, but she and her two-year-old son still lived with her pimp in a housing project in Dallas.

Shirley's situation seemed utterly hopeless. Because she represented income, the pimp literally held her hostage by threatening to kill her little boy if she didn't return home to him. If she didn't bring home enough money, he'd beat her son right in front of her, burning his tender young flesh with cigarettes.

Denny decided to dress up and act like a godless heathen in order to pull the wool over her pimp's eyes. He found his disguise at the Salvation Army thrift store, completely aborting the school's dress code. His ingenious strategy was to act as if he and Shirley had plans to go to the laundromat together. This way, Shirley would have her clothes with her after the rescue. In the getaway car, another soul winner would be waiting to help with the escape.

The escape plan was perfectly prearranged. Everyone was confident it would play out like a scene from an action movie. Denny's character, a street savvy thug, apparently liked hanging out with loose women.

### In his own words...

"Hey dude. Got a smoke?" I asked the pimp. A cigarette came flying through the air. I caught it and popped it in my mouth, letting it dangle.

"Stupid broad's been buggin' me all day. Now I gotta take her to the laundromat. Always something, man."

I was making casual conversation while Shirley and her son were stuffing their belongings into a garbage bag. As they were shuffling their way to the car door, I tossed the cancer stick back to him.

"Yeah. I know what you mean," he said.

Suddenly, the girl in the car cried out, "Hey! What's taking so long? We gotta get outta here!"

The hostages went first, and when I got one foot out the apartment door, the pimp woke up.

"Hey, wait a minute. She just did laundry yesterday."

"Oh, geez," I said, trying to think of what to say next. "That ain't none of my business.

"Something's not right here."

I thought, *How about that? This guy's a prophet. What in the world was she thinking doing her laundry the day before the rescue? Apparently, cleanliness is next to godliness.*

We took a few steps forward, away from the apartment.

"You take another step and you're dead," the pimp informed me.

I turned around and said, "You're right, buddy. You've been had. I'm a preacher and she's a Christian. Your girl's given her life to God and she's gonna live for Jesus now," I said to a guy with a gun pointed at my head.

"Shirley's leaving, man. We're taking her and the boy outta here." I turned and faced the getaway car.

"No," came the reply.

Both women looked at me, wondering what to do next. I shouted, "Get in the car, ladies!"

"Denny, he will kill you. He will!"

"Don't worry about me. Get in the car!"

I took another step, which brought about another menacing death threat.

"You take one more step and I'll kill you."

I took another step.

"No. No. I don't think you will You see, it's not worth it. If you pull the trigger and I die, you're going to prison for at least twenty years and I'll be going to heaven. Then, you're gonna rot in hell because you killed someone and I'll still be in heaven. How do I know this? If you've noticed, I've got a loud voice and I've been using it. All your neighbors are looking out their windows to see what's going on out here. They've seen you with a gun to my head. Now we got plenty of eyewitnesses to send you to prison. No problem, man. You won't have the hooker. I'll be in heaven and you'll be on your way to jail. Is that what you want?"

The pimp didn't say it out loud, but I could hear him thinking, *Oh, man, this guy is right, What do I do now?*

"Listen, I don't want you gettin' jittery, but I'm leaving. If you have a brain in your head, you won't shoot me. But if you do, I want you to know, I'm going to heaven. Now, here I go. I'm gonna move my left foot."

"You take that step and you're a dead man!"

I took two steps.

"You take another step and I'll kill you!"

Six steps later, I heard, "You take any more steps and I'll keeeelll you. You touch that car door and I'll kill you. You open that car door and I'll kill you. You open that car door and you're a dead man! If you start that car, I'll keeeelll you. Turn it off, or I'll kill you. Put it back in park, man, or I'll kill you. Get back in this driveway. You're a dead man!"

No one died and never once did I think, *God, take him out.*

## IN HOSTILE TERRITORY

Another disgruntled pimp hired a professional hitman to kill Denny, but he didn't realize it until one night a very well-dressed man stopped him on the street. He had a feeling he might be looking at trouble.

**In his own words...**

"What's wrong?" I asked him.

"You Denny Nissley?" he asked me.

"Yeah, that's me."

He pulled back one side of his jacket to reveal a huge wad of cash. "I was paid three thousand dollars." My first thought was, *I'd like to have your problems.* Then he opened the other side of his jacket to reveal his shiny 9mm Beretta. "To kill you," he added.

Apparently, I was doing a great job reaching people. *Praise God! Too many Cedar Springs Avenue hookers are being saved.* Then I realized I was staring at a real hitman and there was an actual price on my head. My victorious thought was short-lived. My next thought was, *That's nice, but now I'm scared.*

Although I feared for my life, the peace and security of knowing God's precious promises came flooding in, overtaking the enemy's empty threats against my life.

"Have you prayed about this?" I asked out of the blue.

"What? What did you say to me?" he asked in amazement.

"I said, did you pray about whether or not you should kill me. If you're gonna kill one of God's servants, don't you think you'd better ask God first before you do it?"

His response came stumbling out, "Well, I, ah, ah, well, yeah, maybe. I guess maybe I should."

"You'd better. Think about it. This is serious stuff here. You know how to find me, right? You can kill me any day, isn't that right?"

"Yeah, that's right. Gordon Lindsey Hall, Room 211. Preacher man, Denny Nissley," he said, making sure I knew he knew my name.

When he was done letting me see his gun, he walked away.

I fell to the ground on my knees. *Thank you, Lord. You've spared my life. Now spare his, Lord. Save his soul and let the light of your grace shine tonight, Lord. When he prays, dear God, help him to find Jesus.*

Four days later, the pimp found me on the streets. He did not look happy.

"Kenneth gave back the money," he said, annoyed.

Two things were confirmed. The hitman had a name and it was the disgruntled pimp who wanted me dead.

"So, it was you."

"Yeah, it was. Man, you're lucky. I've seen Kenneth kill someone for twenty-five dollars. But I figured it out. If I mess with you, I mess with God, so I called off the hit."

"Oh," I said. I thought, *That's good news. At least he took my advice.*

"But the next day I saw this guy handing out little pieces of paper at the store, ya know. Whadda ya call 'em? Gospel tracts? Anyway, I asked if he knew you. I figured anyone handing out gospel tracts had to know you. He said he didn't know you. I couldn't believe it. Anyway, he said he knew Jesus and that was what mattered. He told me I could give my life to God and that he would pray for me. So, I prayed with the guy right there and God saved me. Can you believe that? I'm one of youse now," he said with open excitement.

"Praise God! Thank you, Jesus!" Together, we shouted and rejoiced.

"Hey, come here, man," I said, pulling him into the same alley where my last death threat had occurred. "God saved you and now He's gonna fill you with His Holy Spirit."

"Fill me? Fill me with what?"

"Shut up, man. You're gonna love it!"

I laid my hands on the ex-pimp and God filled him with the Holy Spirit. No church service or how-to seminar, just the laying on of hands and the prayer of a Bible school student who had a burden for street people. It's not recorded anywhere but here, or taught in any Bible school, but a revival took place in an alley by a dumpster in Dallas. We uncovered holy ground on a side street.

Afterward, I once again fell to my knees and poured out my gratitude to God for sparing my life and letting me experience the answer to my prayer. What a thrill it was to witness a soul being snatched from the very depths of darkness. It wasn't just any ordinary soul. It was someone who paid Kenneth, the hitman, to exterminate me, the pesky street preacher.

# CAN'T QUIT, WON'T DIE

One particular nude modeling place got thumped on pretty hard by the Holy Ghost hitmen from Christ for the Nations. The seedy business charged twenty dollars to watch twenty minutes of nude modeling. MasterCard and Visa were accepted, but that wasn't satisfactory for the zealous Christians. They were determined not to stop until Jesus was accepted, too. It was a legitimate business in Dallas, but not in the eyes of God.

*In his own words...*

"You Denny Nissley, ain't cha?" the man said in a seriously distinguishable, twangy, Texan accent.

Not everyone in the downtown Dallas red light district knew me by name, but most of them had heard about me. I was the resident street preacher. I made no attempt to hide the fact that I had come to preach the gospel, but what they didn't realize was that I was the leader of a gang of Bible school students bent on destroying their businesses.

"You that street preacher everyone's talkin' 'bout, ain't cha?"

"That's right. I'm Denny, and you are…?"

"I'm Kerry. I manage the place. Someone told me you been prayin' over my buildin'. Whatcha trying to do, get the buildin' saved?" he asked.

He seemed pleased with himself, standing there letting the brim of his faded cowboy hat shade his tanned, thin face.

"No, Kerry, we laid our hands on the building and cursed your business."

"Well, I didn't think Christian were allowed to cuss," he chuckled.

"You don't understand. I said we cursed your business. That means we asked God to make it go bankrupt, so you'd have to go out, get a job, and work by the sweat of your brow like the Bible says. And we asked God to let these women who work to satisfy the lusts of sinful men come out from slavery and accept Jesus as their Savior so they can live for Him."

"Hmmmm. I don't like thaaa….aaat," he said, thoughtfully.

"Well, I didn't think you woooo….uuud," I informed him.

Kerry reached backward into the corner of his raunchy office to grab a 12-gauge, double barreled, sawed-off shotgun. He put two shells in it while I watched, and then planted himself between me and the door.

With the gun to my ear, he cocked the hammer and started to pull back the trigger. I could see Kerry's fingers turning red. Kerry stared at me and withdrew the shotgun to check the safety. He pushed it through the other way, then pointed the gun at my head again. He pulled the trigger, but the hammer would not release.

He was speechless, gazing at me in amazement.

Since there was a standoff going on between him and God, I decided to sing. "The weapons of our warfare are not carnal, but they are mighty in the Holy Ghost..."

Kerry looked at me as if I was crazy. "You're nuts. You're about to die and you're singing Sunday school hymns?"

"Yeah, but I'm not dead now, am I? Look at me. I'm alive!"

This time I had the cocky smile. Kerry put the gun down in defeat. He took a moment to think things through.

"Thanks, Denny. Thanks for praying for my business. Ever since you prayed, business has been doin' real gooo...ood."

"Yeah, but now that you know, it's going under," I said emphatically. I left Kerry alone so he might consider what had just happened.

Saturday nights are the busiest night of the week, so I decided to observe the booming business by going back in and sitting on a couch in the reception area. When a customer sat down beside me, I asked innocently, "Hey, how ya doin'? You come here often?"

Before he could reply, I started to tell him about Jesus.

"What happened? Did this place become a church or sumthin'," he asked before making a hasty exit.

"Not yet," I laughed.

Kerry was livid but extremely curious to find out what made me so bold. He and his girlfriend, who happened to be one of the models, decided they'd take the intended murder victim out for some steak and eggs.

"Hold it. You don't know what they did to this food." I stopped them from gobbling down the diner grub. "Better let a man of God pray over it," I suggested.

"Well, when you put it that way," Kerry's girlfriend said softly.

They looked at each other in a somewhat mesmerized state. I prayed and then shared my testimony. The two irreligious people listened as I showed them how to make things right between them and God.

The day after the failed murder attempt, Kerry took his shotgun out to the country where he shot round after round. There was no doubt in Kerry's mind that my brains should have been blown apart. He knew there was no earthly explanation as to why the gun wouldn't go off just the day before.

The next time I saw Kerry, he asked, "Denny, remember the other night? What do you...ooo think happened?"

I conveyed what I could about the power of God to save, deliver, and restore. Kerry listened, probably out of respect. We developed a friendship over the next few months. I took Kerry to the gym where we played basketball, lifted weights, and went swimming. When the right time came, Kerry accepted my invitation to go to church. He brought his girlfriend, and she brought their son.

I had to break a few Bible school rules and give up some personal time, but it was worth it because a pervert became a saint, and so did a stripper. His girlfriend became his wife and Kerry got out of the nude modeling business and found a real job.

I was more determined than ever to take the love of Jesus to where it was most desperately needed and hardest to find. During my time at Christ for the Nations, I became a God-fearing, devil-hating, Holy Ghost hitman whose heart's desire was to faithfully execute the orders from headquarters—go out into the highways and hedges, and compel the people to come in.

In my case, that meant going into the strip joints of Dallas, Texas.

For Denny Nissley, it was that plain and that simple. Professional hitmen don't normally travel in packs, but during the late 70's, the righteous ones in Dallas did. It wasn't long before the managers who followed Kerry in the nude modeling business got saved and the business had to close its doors. When a similar business tried to open in its place, there were too many strikes by the Holy Ghost hitmen from Christ for the Nations for it to succeed. When the owner of the building got wind of what was going on, he decided to call the street preacher himself.

**In his own words...**

"Hey, you Denny Nissley, that street preacher guy?"

"Yeah, I'm Denny. I've been known to preach on some streets."

"Listen, I gotta know more about this God you've been preaching about."

He sounded distressed.

"Okay, where should meet?"

I thought I was making an appointment to counsel someone in need.

"How about that old strip joint, Live Nude Modeling?"

I was about to meet Ron, the owner of the building. I found out later that Ron had another vocation. He was the leader of the

Dallas chapter of the Hell's Angels biker gang. Meanwhile, I was thrilled at the prospect of ministering to a potential convert. It seemed miraculous that God was doing such great and mighty works on the boulevard. I felt privileged and honored to play a part in this phenomenal move of the Holy Spirit.

The door flung open.

"I'm Ron. Come on in, preacher," he said slowly.

As he stared at me, I couldn't help noticing his beady eyes appeared to have muscles of their own. In his case, looks alone could have killed. It was plain to see he wasn't thrilled about leaving behind whatever sins he had been committing to come hear a sermon. I realized, by the look of things, he had no intention of receiving any counseling. I went in anyway.

Ron shut the door behind him and locked it with a key, which he threw down on a beat-up old coffee table. I sat on the worn-out sofa while the biker wrapped himself around a metal chair he had turned around.

He totally looked and acted the part—Murderer, First, Second and Third Degree.

"Preach to me, mister. And you'd better make it good 'cause it'll be your last sermon."

Much to my surprise, Ron was not the only one in the audience. The devil showed up to let me know he was there to listen in on my session with his disciple. I let fear suffocate my thoughts until I realized there was someone else in attendance.

God assured me He was right there beside me, so I preached the Bible, from Genesis to Maps, front to back. I told Ron everything I ever knew, heard of, or thought about God's plan of salvation.

"So, mister, what do you think?"

"Are you done?" Ron asked in a serious tone.

"Yeah, I'm done."

All the time, I was preaching, I looked for Ron's weapon. He wasn't wearing a jacket, so a gun or a knife would have been hard to hide. I kept thinking, *How's this guy going to kill me?* I forgot the place came equipped with a German Shepherd attack dog with size XL teeth.

Ron summoned his dog. From a back room, his ready-to-please guard dog came charging, full speed down the long corridor. I looked Ron straight in the eyes, pointed to the dog, addressed the devil, and shouted, "Be still in the name of Jesus!"

All of a sudden, everything became still. Only the dog's whimpering interrupted the holy silence. The dog withdrew and collapsed about twenty-five feet from where I was standing.

"All right, mister," I challenged Ron one last time. "You've heard the word of God. You've seen the power of God. It's heaven or hell. Either you turn, or you burn. What'll it be?"

Ron looked at his impotent dog, unlocked the door, and cursed at me as I slowly approached the exit. When we were eyeball to eyeball, nose to nose, he let out a gnarly growl. "Get out!"

I left unharmed, but the devil took quite a beating.

# DIVINE APPOINTMENTS

Seemingly random happenings turn into divine appointments, that is if you're Denny Nissley. After leaving Bible school, Denny experienced several crucial turning points. A series of incidents helped shape his unwavering commitment to follow the leading of the Holy Spirit, no matter what. Denny lets God set the appointment book because things work out when God is in charge.

If Denny does something extraordinary and outrageous for God, it's not because he has some great talent or wonderful confidence in his abilities. It's simply because Denny is willing to let God to work through him, and that's precisely why amazing things keep happening in his ministry.

Denny was in a restaurant in Greeley, Colorado when God laid it on his heart to stand up and preach. At first, he argued with God, telling Him, *Lord, you've got to be kidding!* Nevertheless, he preached, and everyone stopped what they were doing. The dishwasher stopped washing dishes. The manager stopped managing. Customers stopped eating. The mashed potatoes got cold, and the ice cream melted.

. . .

*In his own words...*

Once the manager got over the shock of having a stray street preacher in his restaurant, he walked toward me as if he was going to take control. I looked at him pointed my finger, and said, "Hold on. I'm not finished." Unfortunately for the manager, I hadn't had an altar call yet.

"Folks, if you're in here and you don't believe what I'm saying, ask God, and He will make Himself real to you."

A man stood up and said, "Preacher, I've got a bad back. What's your God gonna do about that?"

Instantly, I was drenched with the power of God. "Sir, God told me your one leg is too short. Now, sit down," I instructed the skeptic.

"Are you his wife?" I asked the woman sitting next to him.

"Well, yes," she answered, not knowing what else to do.

"Come here. Hold his legs up."

"See that?" I exclaimed. "One of your legs is at least a couple of inches too short!"

By this time the everyone in the restaurant wanted to see this poor man's short leg. After the crowd had gathered around, I gently laid my hand on her shoulder, not his, and prayed. The customers, the dishwasher, and the manager all witnessed the man's leg grow. His wife thought she was hallucinating and dropped his leg.

The man stood up and shouted, "I'm healed!"

It was obvious to everyone that the man was healed because one of his pant legs was way too short. I asked his wife, "Ma'am, why is his one pant leg too short?"

She stuttered in disbelief, "I guess, preacher, because I, ah, I hemmed it up because his one leg used to be too short!"

"Is that right?" I asked.

A man gave his life to the Lord and got healed. A woman rededicated her life to the Lord and got baptized in the Holy Ghost. Another woman asked me to pray for her because she had bursitis and arthritis. We prayed, all right We had "Church-it-is" that day, right there in the restaurant in Greeley because I let God be in charge.

But then I went home and someone came to visit me. The devil invaded my victory party to tell me I was a jerk. *You might as well pack your back and leave town. You're going to be labeled a nutcase. What are you doing preaching in a public place, you fool? Nobody's going to let you come and minister at their church.*

The devil tormented me. I felt as if I was burried beneath the valley instead of coming off a glorious mountaintop. *Where are you, Lord? How come I feel so rotten?* And then I heard God's voice tenderly speaking to my heart.

*Go ask that man who was healed if he thinks you're a jerk. Ask the man whose sins were forgiven today if he thinks you're a jerk. Ask the women who got filled with my Spirit if she thinks you ought to pack your bags and leave town. Ask me on Judgment Day what I think about your obedience.*

Not a jerk. Just enough on fire for the Lord to obey his promptings.

~

EAT OR PRAY

In a different restaurant in another state, Denny stumbled upon another opportunity to obey the Holy Spirit. He came out of the restroom and a man was having an epileptic seizure, right in front of him. The poor man was convulsing, so Denny grabbed him by the waist and started praying.

"God heal this man. Take your hands off this man, devil! Let him alone. Be healed in Jesus' name."

He didn't make any attempt to restrain his voice. He purposely kept his eyes closed. He didn't want to see what might have been going on around him.

**In his own words...**

All of a sudden, I felt a big cumbersome hand on my shoulder, and thought, *Oh, good. I've got some agreement going on here.* So, I kept praying until I felt the man had been released. When I opened my eyes, I knew God had touched him.

"Are you all right?" I asked the man on the floor.

"Yes, I am, thanks," he replied.

I looked over my shoulder and saw the owner of the big arm I had felt earlier.

"Hi, there. Are you a Christian?" I asked.

"I'm the manager," answered the man in an unfriendly tone.

"Ah, huh."

I knew there would be more in this declaration.

"You can't pray in my restaurant," he informed me.

"What?"

I couldn't believe his reaction. It was plain to see the man having the seizure was glad I had prayed.

"He was having…" I tried to inject a statement.

"I don't care what he was having. You don't pray in my restaurant. It's a restaurant, not a church."

"What? God just helped this man!" I thought for a moment, and said, "Okay, then, let's suppose you're having a heart attack. You've got two breaths left in you. Here come the paramedics. They've backed up the ambulance to the door and they're bring in the equipment. I suppose you would want me to stop them. Stop! This isn't a hospital. It's a restaurant."

The way he glared at me, I thought I might be going to the hospital by the time this was over, but I continued anyway. "You know, mister manager, you're right. But I don't want anyone to die because this is a restaurant and not a church. And for your information, I am the church because where I go, Jesus goes."

"Don't pray in my restaurant," was all he could say.

"Fine. Don't eat in church."

## DADDY'S GIRLS

Jesus has a special relationship with children. He can use them to reach lost souls, and perhaps it is their child-like faith that makes sharing the gospel easier than it is for adults.

> *Like arrows in the hands of a warrior are children born in one's youth.*
> *Blessed is the man whose quiver is full of them. They will not be put to*

*shame when then contend with their enemies in the gate.* Psalm
127:4-5

It should come as no surprise that the Nissley children are great
"warrior arrows" for the Lord. They've learned by example how
to follow God's leading. The following story is just one example
of how the Nissley-ettes are instrumental when it comes to
taking the love of Jesus to where it's most desperately needed and
hardest to find.

### In his own words...

We stopped to get a bite to eat in Silverdale, Washington. At the
time, we had five children. We had to wait patiently as we made
our way through the roped off maze to get to the counter to
place our order. We happened to be in line behind an older man
pushing a woman in a wheelchair. She had a hard time deciding
what she wanted to eat, but eventually settled on the salad bar.

Everyone in the restaurant, including my family, couldn't refrain
from looking at the salad bar area when the women in the
wheelchair started to have a nervous fit. Her husband tried to
pacify her the best he could.

He gently asked, "Dear, would you care for some carrots on your
salad?"

"Carrots! What?"

You could tell she was deeply distressed by the mere mention of
the vegetable.

"Yes. No. I mean, I don't know!" she answered with disgust. "I
can't believe I'm here without my nerve pills. How come you
brought me here without my nerve pills? What about my
medication? Give me celery. No. Give me carrots. No onions. I

don't want that! Why'd you give me that? What am I going to do?"

My family watched as the poor man was publicly humiliated. Finally, he wheeled her to a table and went to get his salad. All five girls agreed when one of them pointed out, "Daddy, that lady needs Jesus."

"And she's fixin' to get Him, girls," I assured them.

As the man went for his salad, I thought I'd take advantage of the moment.

"Ma'am, I could help noticing something. You're having a real hard time today, aren't you? I'm a minister. I wonder, would it be okay if I prayed with you? Jesus wants to help you, ma'am. Could I pray for you?"

I was waiting for a cane to come flying out from behind the wheelchair. The devil told me, *This will be historic. You're going to get arrested for badgering an old lady in a wheelchair. There goes your ministry.*

When I realized the devil didn't want me to do it, I figured God did.

"That would be nice. I'm a Christian, too," she said slowly.

"I want you to know something. I know what it's like to feel as if any moment you could lose your mind and never get it back. I also want you to know that Jesus healed my mind. He restored me completely, and since then, I've experienced more peace in this world than I ever imagined existed."

Tears were streaming down her cheeks. Everyone watched as I prayed for the distraught woman. I held her hand and offered a nice general 'chill out' prayer.

"What are you doing?" her husband asked, rushing to her side. His lower jaw had bottomed out with alarm when he saw me with her.

"Thank you, Reverend. I feel so much better. Be quiet, dear. He prayed for me. I'm going to be okay."

Her husband's anguish started to abate. "I've never seen her so exasperated, and now look at her. She's so peaceful...without her medication," he admitted.

"None of our ministers ever prayed like that," she confessed. "You know, I don't get out often, and I never get to be with children," she said softly as she eyed the Nissley-ettes.

"We had one son, but he died when he was only five. I couldn't have more, so I don't have grandchildren. So, you see, I don't get to hug any children. Nowadays you have to be so careful about touching children. Innocent people can get accused of doing bad things to children."

She looked saddened by that fact.

"Well, we have plenty of kids. You can hug on 'em as much as you want!"

As if on cue, the girls came running over to their table. Leah tried her two-year-old best to climb up to get a hug. The image of our toddler's sneakers jammed in the spokes of the woman's wheelchair will be engraved in my mind forever. Rachel, Bethany, Melody, Deborah, and Leah each took turns hugging and loving on the lady who needed Jesus.

# TURNING POINTS

I don't know about you, but I'm energized when God puts me with Christians who are completely sold out for the sake of His kingdom. I feel sorry for Christians who haven't relinquished it all to God. They don't know what they're missing, but I do because I've seen what happens when God is in charge.

While strolling around the historic district of St. Louis, Missouri, Denny and a couple of friends spotted a group of nuns. Since nuns are generally admired for their godly devotion, Denny and friends stopped to talk with the sisters. The majesty of God was the topic of their friendly conversation. The nuns appeared to be interested in what Denny does, so he told them about his upcoming outreach event. Before long, a small group of curious tourists had gathered to listen in.

When the group formed a snug circle for a word of prayer, a man from the street asked if he could join the prayer huddle. When he started praying, the glory of God fell upon the scene. For about fifteen minutes, the group experienced heaven on earth as they became immersed in God's majestic presence. For them, it was just another normal day. A bunch of God's kids talking to Abba, Heavenly Father. What's the big deal?

Whenever a crowd of curious people have gathered, Denny can't help himself. He had to preach, especially after their spirit-filled prayer meeting. The nuns looked as if they were about to fly away. They had never been in a charismatic meeting.

"I wish the power of God would take over our prayer meetings as it has the street of St. Louis!" one of the sisters confided.

The nuns continued to watch in awe as God ministered to people on the streets. Denny thought it was interesting that the man from the streets, who could easily have been mistaken for a bum, had prayed with so much power and might. He turned out to be someone Denny met in Dallas when he was a student at Christ for the Nations. Brother Matthew had a long history of winning at least three people a day to Christ, not from a pulpit, but on the streets.

During that day, Denny rediscovered the fact that when God is given complete control, His accomplishments and results far exceed what we can achieve on our own.

The Bible says we can do nothing apart from Him, and like Denny likes to say, "Apart from Him, we should do nothing."

## A TURNING POINT

The importance of doing the Lord's will was reinforced for Denny one afternoon when he and Sandy, only recently married, pulled up to a convenience store on the outskirts of at the city where he was scheduled to preach later that night. Two teenaged boys were in the middle of a boisterous fistfight. People stood around gasping as the Anglo and Mexican teens locked horns. The two were having it out tooth and nail, both bent on winning.

. . .

***In his own words...***

I shoved the gearshift into park and told Sandy, "I feel as if the Lord told me to preach to break up the fight."

"Well, Denny?" She said matter-of-factly.

I jumped out of the van and started toward the boys just as another man stepped out from the crowd and successfully pulled the boys apart and broke up the fight.

"Go home, everyone. This is over," the man informed the crowd.

I got back in the van and Sandy looked at me funny and said, "Didn't you say the Lord told you to preach?"

I thought about my wife's questions and immediately began to rationalize my excuse. "Well, it was just to break up the fight and now there's nothing to break up."

"Oh, I thought that if the Lord told you to preach, He might have wanted you to preach."

I felt convicted but not for long. There was nothing I could do. There was no one left to preach to, so we left.

Later that evening, Sandy and I were getting ready to order our meal at a restaurant when we discovered our waitress had been crying. Her puffy eyes and the expression on her face exposed her sorrow, so I told her I was a minister and offered my support.

"Oh, praise the Lord. It's my nephew. You see, a Mexican boy shot and killed my nephew today. They started fighting at a convenience store."

Our ears perked up. My throat began to go shut. My eyes welled up with hot tears. Sandy and I knew what she was about to tell us. I reached out to grab ahold of my wife's hand.

"After the fight, the Mexican boy found my nephew at the edge of town, got a gun, and shot him. It's so sad, so unnecessary."

She looked at me intently. At this point, it was obvious I was deeply affected by what she was saying. She stared at me as if to say, *There, there, Preacher. It'll be all right. I'm going to be okay.*

There was nothing much we could do or say. I didn't know how deeply I was affected until my anguish came out while preaching that night. Out of my heartache, I told the congregation about the teenager who died, perhaps because I didn't obey God.

"I was there and felt as if God told me to preach to break up the fight, but I didn't because someone else broke up the fight. Only God knows what would have happened if I had preached. Please don't misunderstand. I know God hasn't given His throne over to me. God is quite capable of saving lives and souls and accomplishing His will without my help. Nevertheless, I know now that obedience is required on a moment-to-moment basis... that is, in God's plan for my life. How about you? Are you willing to obey God at a moment's notice?"

The Lord used that senseless tragedy as a turning point in my ministry. Many times since that day, when I receive a prompting from God to do something, and I start thinking that I really don't feel like it, I immediately remember the waitress with the puffy eyes and her nephew, the boy who died because of a dispute that took place in a convenience store's parking lot.

# GOD'S SPECIAL FORCES

Outreach events with street preachers are often life changing and unforgettable. Unexpected events may take place but never come as a surprise when Denny Nissley's in town.

One Sunday evening, evangelist Jonathan Gainsbrugh and Denny were scheduled to preach at the same church at the same time. Denny was told it was a clerical error, but he knew better. God doesn't make mistakes. It was decided Jonathan would preach that night at the 91st Psalm Church.

Near the end of his message, Jonathan turned to Denny and said, "Brother Nissley, you know what I'm thinking?" He paused. "I'm thinking I'm pretty thirsty after having preached and everything. You thirsty, brother?"

***In his own words...***

I didn't know exactly where Brother Gainbrugh was going with this, but I knew I should say yes. "Ya know, Brother Gainsbrugh, I do believe I'm thirsty now that you mention it."

"Well, maybe we oughta go get a drink somewhere after service," he said casually.

Then it dawned on me. I knew where he was going. I also knew where we were going after church.

"Yes, sir. Might I suggest we go out for some afterglow fellowship?" I said without much emotion. About two hundred people in the congregation listened in on our conversation.

"Yeah, that's it. That's what I had in mind, Brother Nissley. Anybody interested in joining us for a little afterglow fellowship? I saw Sonny's Bar and Grille down the road a'ways. How 'bout we go there and get us a cold one?"

"Fine with me, Brother Gainsbrugh. Let's go on and do that."

The church people looked at each other. No one knew quite what to say. Perhaps they were thinking, *Oops. These traveling evangelists aren't what we expected.*

Then Jonathan asked the congregation, "How many want to go to Sonny's with me and Brother Denny?"

No one said or did anything, so I stepped up to the pulpit.

"Aw, look here," I said pointing to the congregation. "No one wants to go with us. They don't want to win this city for Christ. They just want to hear about it. Doesn't look as if they want to find some lost souls and bring 'em to Christ...at least not tonight."

"Okay, folks, I'll tell ya what," Jonathan explained. "Brother Denny and I are going to have a drink at Sonny's. We'll go and we'll make a stand for the Lord down at Sonny's. How many of you want to come along?"

Some folks got the gist of what was developing. Eight people raised their hands when the pastor got energized and spoke out.

"No way! We're not going down to Sonny's to make a stand for Jesus with ten people from my church. We ain't gonna do that. You wanna make a stand for Jesus, Brother Gainsbrugh, you're gonna have to take a whole lot more of us, I'm going with you. Anyone else want to get past the humdrum boring part of your Christian faith?"

"I got kids. I can't go," someone called out.

"My husband and I will stay behind and watch the kids in the nursery," someone else called out.

Except for the nursery volunteers and the children, a majority of the two hundred church members went to Sonny's for a drink, equipped with the gospel and some instructions.

"Listen up. Sonny's a drinking establishment, therefore, we're going to be paying customers. Order a Coke and don't hesitate to leave the server a tip. Don't worry. You'll know what to do when we get there. Smile. Smile a lot. Don't preach. Don't pass out tracts. Don't do anything unless you get the word from us."

## GOD IN THE PUB

I talked to the owner when we arrived. "Listen. There's a bunch of us out here and we're real thirsty. We were wondering if we could come in and have a drink. The only thing is, there's a mess of us out here."

The owner looked delighted. "Sure thing, but we don't have any servers on duty except for one, and there's the bartender and me."

"We could get our own drinks at the bar, if that's all right," I said.

"Oh, okay," she replied.

I went outside and gave the orders.

"All right, now, listen up. They don't have but one server, so trickle on up to the bar and get yourself a drink."

The pastor and the church secretary led the procession. They were among the first to enter the cocktail lounge. The rest of the dehydrated filed in after them. Three women at the bar, startled by the oncoming entourage, showed visible signs of shock when they saw their pastor along with most of his congregation approaching.

It was a grand time of fellowship, everyone sipping Cokes at Sonny's—us and the usual forty or so Sunday night customers. At this point, no one suspected a church group had infiltrated the local hangout except for one patron. She grabbed the church secretary and whispered in her ear, "Lola, call us tomorrow. We'll get right with God."

With that, she signaled her gal pals and the wayward church ladies slipped out the back door. Jonathan put two fingers in his mouth and let out a country whistle.

"Hey, everyone! I want y'all to sing Happy Birthday to my friend Denny."

It wasn't my birthday and Jonathan didn't say it was. He just asked everyone to sing and the bar flies happily agreed.

I played along. "Oh, golly. Stop it. You're embarrassing me."

After the song Jonathan started in with, "Speech! Speech! Let's hear from the birthday boy. How 'bout it, Denny?"

"Oh, no, no. You guys! What in the world can I say?" I asked, knowing exactly what I was going to say.

"Oh, okay. Thank you so much. I guess I should tell you about another birthday I had that was way more important than any other day in my life 'cause I haven't been the same since that day. It was the day I was born again. Twelve hundred pounds of compressed cardboard fell on my leg. The doctors wanted to amputate. Then in 1977, I let someone talk me into going to a church service...."

I preached a bit until the crowd caught on and got angry.

"Shut up, man! Give it a rest! No preaching!" the barmaid shouted.

"Hey, cut it out, man. I'm Jewish!" another lady exclaimed.

I turned around and looked at her and said, "So was Jesus, and He died for Jews and Gentiles alike."

The roar of the crowd was getting louder until Jonathan starting singing, "God's not dead. He's alive! NO! NO! NO! God's not dead!"

It wasn't long until the church members joined in. An irate man started pumping the jukebox full of quarters and turned the volume way up, trying to drown us out. A bunch of Christians gathered around the jukebox and sang their hearts out, "God's not dead, He is alive! NO! NO! NO! God's not dead!"

Jonathan and I retreated toward the back door to watch the action. The 91st Psalmers rejoiced, greatly. The majority at Sonny's was having a great time. The minority looked either confused, angry, or intrigued. Jonathan and I looked at each other and realized we had successfully launched an entire church into bar evangelism.

Just then the back door opened, and a policeman walked in. He looked at Jonathan and asked, "What's going on here?"

Jonathan took a sip of his Coke and said, "Well, sir, I'm not sure, but it looks to me as though these folks are having church."

"Aw, for crying out loud. All right, who's in charge here?" the police officer asked in a loud voice.

"Personally, officer," Jonathan looked around, took another sip, and said, "I think I'd have to say it's the Holy Spirit."

The officer knew he wasn't getting anywhere with Jonathan, so he turned, put his finger on my chest, and said, "You! Come with me." I obeyed.

"What's going on here?" he asked after we were outside.

"I'm not sure, but I think those people in there are having church," I answered politely.

"Yeah, I heard that. But I gotta know who's in charge, and don't tell me the Holy Spirit is in charge!"

"Well, sir, I gotta be honest with you. Whatever He's not in charge of, I don't want any part of."

He looked at me with his head cocked sideways. "You're in charge, aren't you?"

"No, sir. It's not me. Look around. I'm not in charge."

I looked across the parking lot. A half dozen squad cars faced the bar. Someone must have called the police to report a riot because officers in riot gear surrounded the place, ready and waiting for orders from their commander to squash the spirited celebration.

"You'd better stop them," he told me.

"Hey, I am not in charge. How am I going to stop those people from singing and having a good time?"

"I'm telling you…we'll go in there and get them out one at a time if you don't do something," the officer in charge threatened.

About that time, a few guys from the church walked out the back door. One of them worked at the police station.

"Hey, Joe. Come here. What's going on in there?" the frustrated officer asked his colleague.

"Oh, hey, Sergeant. We're just having fun." Joe replied.

"You're with them?"

"Yup."

The sergeant pointed at me and said, "Tell this guy to call them off."

"Look. I think you'd better handle this yourself," Joe said.

"Come on, Joe. Help us out here. We can't, ah, we don't know what to do," the sergeant pleaded with his fellow officer.

He sounded desperate, so I stepped in. "Don't worry. We'll go. We're having a little afterglow fellowship, but we're done."

I got everyone's attention and told the crowd, "We've been asked by the police to leave, so everyone go on home now."

The church people humbly left the bar, repeating the chorus softly under their breath as the riot police held the door open. For some reason, when the congregation saw police cars in the parking lot, everyone suddenly got enthusiastic about bar evangelism.

"Now what, brother Denny? Where to?" they asked with excitement.

"We're done. Go on home."

The pastor, associate pastor, Brother Jonathan, and I were about to leave when the owner came running out the door. "Wait! Pastor! Ummm, we need you to come back inside."

We went back in to discover the server and the barmaid standing there, their hands dripping with money.

"Your people left this laying on the tables," the owner said.

"That's a tip," the pastor explained. "They wanted to bless you. They love you and that's yours."

"We don't want their money," the barmaid said. The atmosphere had changed. Guilt filled the air. "It's theirs, not ours."

"God loves you, and if they left it, He wants you to have it."

The server spoke next. "We can't keep it. Would you take it and put it in the offering, pastor?"

"I'll tell you what. Why don't you come to church and you can put it in the offering? We can't touch that money. It's yours."

As we were leaving, the sergeant followed us to ask one more question. "Where are you from? Are you going downtown? Tell me which bar."

I tried to tell him we were done but he didn't believe me.

"Look. We just want to know so we can be prepared, that's all."

"Good night, Sergeant."

The next day the church phone rang off the hook with calls from church members looking to find out the date, time, and location for the next afterglow fellowship.

## GOD'S SPECIAL FORCES

The following Sunday, after one night of bar evangelism, the pastor, a former Hollywood pimp and Green Beret, asked his congregation, "How many of you want to have an impact on this city for God?"

A scattering of voices cried out.

"How many would be willing to quit your job to have an impact on this city? Stand up if you're willing. Who's willing to quit their job to claim this city for God? Who's willing to minister full-time for one full year? Stand up right where you are. Who among us can trust God to supernaturally meet their needs for one year?"

Twelve men stood up. Twelve guys quit their jobs that Sunday to go into the ministry, and that's how the pastor started his evangelism program called God's Special Forces.

"Here's what we're going to do. You men who stood up, you're going to come to this church for six days of prayer. You'll also be fasting. We're all going to fast and pray. We're going to memorize scripture. We're going to know the Word of God. For those of you who didn't, or couldn't stand up, we're going to ask you to double or triple your tithe. This church is going to give these twelve men salaries to evangelize our community. The people in this church are going to pay for these men to make a stand for Jesus."

People all over the congregation stood up to say, "I'll do it," or "I have X number of dollars set aside," or "We were going to purchase a new car, but as of tonight, that money goes to God's Special Forces. We'll keep our old jalopy for one more year!"

In one day, the 91st Psalm Church raised enough money to put twelve men into full-time ministry. When the year was over, every human being in that city had heard the gospel to the point where residents posted signs on their doors: No 91st Psalmers, Jehovah's Witnesses, or Mormons!

God got top billing because, of course, He was in charge.

# SATAN'S WORST NIGHTMARE

E vil exists and has a plan, but God always has a better one. What you'll read in the next couple of chapters will shock you. Some of what is recorded here reads like a horror novel. It seems unbelievable, however, don't be deceived into doubting the authenticity of what took place. Denny continually contends with evil, which makes him one of satan's worst nightmares, as you're about to find out.

The events chronicled here occurred over a two-year period and revolved around a Christ in Action outreach organized in Key West, Florida in 1987. A hundred or so soul winners joined Denny and his preacher buddies at a church for the purposes of hitting the streets to talk to people about Jesus during the city's Halloween festival.

Strange things happened as Denny prepared to take Sandy and the children to Key West's 1987 Fantasy Festival Halloween outreach. For the first time in the ministry's history, things did not work out for Sandy and the children to go to the outreach. At the time, there were three kids and one on the way. Plans flew apart and circumstances dictated that Denny's family would have to stay behind.

Denny knew that God had called him to a ten-day water only fast, and while he didn't know exactly why, he was sure God meant business. It took two years to unravel the mystery behind God's strict requirement and to fully understand the reason circumstances were what they were that particular year.

*In his own words...*

Years before this particular Fantasy Festival outreach, a battered old hearse caught my attention and instantly became a part of our vision for ministry. To me, it was crystal clear. God wanted Christ in Action to own and restore the dreary funeral car, a 1971 Cadillac hearse. When God gave me those instructions, I didn't have the complete explanation. I only knew God would bless the ministry as I continued to obey His peculiar requests.

Twenty-six coats of shiny black lacquer were not enough to satisfy my friend, Ed Campbell, whom God brought into our lives that same year. It would take one more coat to bring the hearse to the point where Ed felt it would be good enough for Christ in Action. God knew I didn't have the skills to transform the old car into a spit-shined parade vehicle and witnessing machine for Jesus, but Ed did.

## COMPLETE OBEDIENCE

Some people live to celebrate Halloween, especially in the city of Key West, Florida. Fantasy Festival is the city's attempt to host a fun-filled time of make-believe for all who might come to frolic. In keeping with the mood of the celebration, Christ in Action showed up with the shiny black funeral car, a sepulcher on wheels, along with a hundred soul winners from all over America. As we suspected from the beginning, it was destined to be a rare event.

The entire team went through an unusually intense time of prayer and spiritual warfare, which was the first definite clue that something profound was about to unfold. During the morning time of prayer, several Christians indicated they felt God wanted His people to go to certain areas of the city at certain times and to stay away from certain areas altogether. They also had very strong feelings that our people were to be off the streets by a particular time.

Because these Christians sensed urgency within God's message, they were willing to be completely obedient. As a result, the most unexpected and amazing turn of events took place. These unusual episodes weren't caught on film by the media, but they were etched in the hearts and minds of people, and most importantly, in the Lamb's Book of Life.

Our fear-inspiring hearse was entered as a float, an entirely appropriate display for Fantasy Festival's Halloween parade. It was well received until we arrived at the judges' stand. The crowd did not like our DON'T BE CAUGHT DEAD WITHOUT JESUS sign that was plastered over the back window of the hearse. ETERNITY WILL BE HELL WITHOUT JESUS appeared on both side windows. Christ in Action's messages for the day were not welcomed.

Six pallbearers wearing tuxedos and dark glasses walked behind the hearse while I drove. The CIA team looked like a pack of spooky Blues Brothers, which was great because they captured the crowd's attention. Naturally, there was a casket inside the hearse. The metal box did not contain a creepy corpse. It came with a very alive street preacher.

"Look everyone! They're stopping," the parade announcer pointed out. "There's something very...well, here's something to see, folks. What is that? It appears, ladies and gentlemen, there's a casket coming out of the hearse. Wait! It looks like they're going to open it. Why would they do that? What could...? Oh! Look! There's someone...," the announcer's tone suddenly changed.

"Ugh, there's someone preaching." She made no attempt to hide her feelings. It was easy to tell that she was thoroughly disgusted.

With a powerful handheld public address system known as a half-mile hailer, the resurrected corpse started his horrifying presentation.

"Standing in front of the judges' stand reminds me that one day we will all stand before God Almighty, the judge of all judges. He's the one we should fear. To fear God is the beginning of wisdom. Are you wise enough to acknowledge the one who can judge whether or not your heart is in right standing with Him? Will you...?"

I had done my homework and checked in with their parade officials. They informed me that parade entries were permitted to do a two to three-minute routine or presentation while in front of the judges, so I told my preacher to plan on giving the listening audience a three-minute shock treatment. Thirty seconds into the routine a police officer began tapping vigorously on the driver's side window. I could feel him screaming at me, but I didn't look at him. I was determined to let the full three minutes go by.

"You can't do this! Get this thing out of here! Hey, do you hear me? I said get this thing outta here! If you don't move this thing, I'm going to get a tow truck in here and haul you away! Now move it!"

He ranted and raved while I looked at my watch and checked the rearview mirror to see if the casket had been returned to the hearse. When it was safely secured, I rolled down the window.

"Oh, I'm sorry. Did you want me to move?"

By this time, the policeman was blistering mad. He looked as if he was going to explode.

"All righty then. We're outta here. Have a nice day, officer!"

With that, I pulled away.

For the grand finale, fifty Christians buried in the crowd whipped out signs, placards, and giant foam hands with the pointing index finger—the kind sports fans bring to cheer on their favorite team. Ours were imprinted with *Jesus is #1.* The entire group then filed in by rank behind the hearse and the entourage retreated into the distance.

Judging by the crowd's animosity, I decided that the hearse would have to go into hiding. We took the long way back to the church where the group was staying and camouflaged it when we arrived. But the outreach had only just begun. It was time for our soul winners to go out on the streets and talk to people about Jesus.


## SPIRITED HALLOWEEN HARASSMENT

It came as no great shock when the police started to pester the outspoken Christians on the streets. However, the intensity of their harassment seemed exceptional. In one instance, a man preached a message of hope and salvation on a street corner while his partner handed out "What's Wrong with Halloween" testimony tracts to people passing by.

"Hey. I want you to know if that guy doesn't stop what he's doing, you're going to jail," a police officer declared to the young man handing out tracts.

"So, if I rob a bank, you're going to arrest that guy over there?" the soul winner asked politely.

The harassment got so severe that I felt it was time to confront the chief of police. When I arrived at police headquarters, I waited longer than most people would because I was determined to question him. I waited patiently until he agreed to see me.

"Your police officers are harassing us, and I'm not going to put up with it. Could you please tell me which law we've broken?" I asked.

The chief of police wouldn't respond until I gave him the name and phone number of Christ in Action's attorney.

"We've successfully sued another city right here in your state, and we'll sue you as well if you don't get off our backs. I guarantee you; you will hear from my lawyer. I've studied the laws that pertain to what we're doing here, and we're not breaking any. If one of your officers find that someone from our group is breaking the law, I want you to contact me," I said, handing him my business card. "I give you my word, I'll deal with them more severely than you would. Do you understand? Now, I suggest you let us go on doing what we're doing, and you will have saved this city a lot of money."

## MIDNIGHT, OCTOBER 31

Three days later, on Halloween night, I took a team of Christians for a time of casual praise and worship on a street that had been blocked off to accommodate pedestrian traffic during Fantasy Festival. It didn't take long for what looked like a majority of the police force to show up with a brigade of paddy wagons. We were surrounded on three of four sides. The team knew I wanted them on their knees. If the righteous were going to be hauled away for praising God in public, then I wanted the righteous to make it difficult.

I held the microphone and started preaching the message I felt God had given me for the citizens of Key West. A crowd had gathered to see what was going on. Naturally, I ended with an alar call.

"Folks, a lot of you out there are attracted to the bizarre and occult nature of this pagan holiday called Halloween when what you should be looking for and celebrating is Jesus, the Lord of lords and the Light of this world. Won't you give your life to Him? He died a bloody death for you. Talk about bizarre. Jesus spooked everyone when He didn't stay dead!"

Afterward, the chief of police came over and said, "Reverend Nissley, are you done?"

"Yeah, I'm done Can I ask you a question? Why'd you bring all those paddy wagons?"

"When I heard you guys were having a religious rally on Halloween night, I thought there might be problems. I brought the wagons in case anyone gave you a hard time. We were prepared to haul them away. We're here to make sure you have your right to preach the gospel in Key West, Reverend Nissley."

# STEALING SATAN'S GOODS

By the next day, the city of Key West started to return to normal. People put away their spooky costumes and went back to their normal routines. The hordes of visitors returned to their hometowns, including a man from Anchorage, Alaska, his wife, and their 24-year-old, pregnant, unmarried daughter.

The man from Alaska was the third-ranking man in the Satanic Church. The daughter, who was four months pregnant, carried her father's baby in her womb. The infant had been conceived with one purpose in mind, and that was to become the next Most Unholy High Sacrifice for the Satanic Church.

The satanic priest had come to Florida to lead a satanic conference over Halloween. Unbeknownst to the Christ in Action team, there were hundreds of satanists in town during Fantasy Festival. They were there with the expressed purposed of opposing Christian influences. In fact, they had been specifically instructed to haunt soul winners and to intrude on Christian activities.

· · ·

*In his own words...*

But a strange thing happened. The devil worshippers could not find one single Christian. They never came in contact with any Christians when they went out on the street looking for them because the Christians were mysteriously absent. Remember that God had explicitly directed our group to be at specific locations at specific times as well as to avoid specific places at other times.

Then the satanists discharged a team in the middle of the night early in Fantasy Festival to go to the church where we were staying to cast spells on God's people. That was the plan until they came down United Street and attempted to cross the street. There was no perceivable obstruction or visible barrier, but when they tried to go toward the church they were supernaturally restrained and physically unable to cross the street or leave the sidewalk on the other side.

They left confused and infuriated. Not willing to give up, they tried again the next night. The same thing happened.

As the festivities started breaking up, even the satanists had to get back to their jobs. When the priest found out that the cursing of God's church didn't take place, he became so furious he decided to return to Florida, taking his wife and daughter with him. They checked into a motel and went to United Street at midnight, searching for the church where the Christ in Action teams had stayed. He looked forward to invoking his master's avenging powers, but much to his surprise, when he stood across the street from the church and attempted to go forward, he couldn't cross the street either!

He tried with all his might to do this simple task, but he, too, was mysteriously restrained and physically unable to leave the sidewalk. After several attempts to cross the street, fraught with hellish anger, he ordered his family back to the motel. Seething and raving like a madman, he scared his own family. His daughter's attempts to calm him down were in vain.

"Father, you're way too angry. You've got to chill out!" she said as she took off to go for a walk.

## SWITCHING SIDES

The priest's daughter walked around the outskirts of Key West only to end up back on United Street. There, she saw a light in a second-floor apartment window near the church, and for that reason, she crossed the street without a problem.

"Hello?" She introduced herself to the church's youth pastor and his wife who happened to live in that apartment and happened to be up at that late hour. They invited her to come inside.

"I've got to tell you something. Please believe me when I tell you this. My father is the most powerful man I've ever known. You must understand something. Whatever, and I mean whatever my father wants, my father gets," she said as she cradled her slightly swollen belly. "In my whole life, I've never seen him fail at anything."

She proceeded to share how there was an invisible wall at the sidewalk across the street and how the devil worshippers' frustrated attempts to interfere with the concealed Christians failed.

"Except this church and that group of Christians, my father has always gotten everything he's ever wanted. I know now that God has more power than satan does. I want to serve God," she concluded.

The satanic priest's daughter gave her life to the Lord that night in the youth pastor's living room. They had a time of deliverance, casting out the demons she had grown up with, probably since before birth. They prayed and dedicated the baby in her womb to Jesus, and before the sun came up, the woman left Key West to go into hiding under a fictions name.

Inevitably, the people involved in that particular Fantasy Festival outreach quickly rose to first position on the devil's TOP TEN HIT LIST after brazenly stealing his Most High Unholy Sacrifice.

## ONE YEAR LATER

The Fantasy Festival outreach was schedule for October of the following year; however, things were not normal. Once again, Denny's family was prevented from going.

The host church in Key West received a call from someone on staff at Bob Larson's Answer Man show. The caller said he wanted to notify the church leaders that Anton LaVey, the founder of the Satanic Church and the author of the Satanic Bible, had called in to the show and mentioned the church specifically. He felt that LaVey's comments could be construed as a hostile threat, so he decided to forward the information.

The pastor of the church called another minister who was instrumental in helping organize the outreach who then called Christ in Action's office to tell Denny about the devil's attempt to intimidate them. LaVey had mentioned last year's Halloween conference on Larson's show. He intimated that his group had experienced some setbacks, but things were looking better for this year's meeting. LaVey had said something to the effect of, "You tell those people, I want them to know this year I'm not sending a boy to do a man's job."

· · ·

*In his own words...*

I came up with a message of my own. I figured if the devil had my picture circulating in his ranks, I would do the same. I made sure every Christian at the outreach saw a mugshot of LaVey's face.

"Hey, gang," I said, holding up the photo. "This guy will be in the crowd, and he needs Jesus. Don't be afraid of him. Cast the devil out of him."

That was my message to the soul winners. And, once again, I told them to fast and pray. Three days into the outreach, two soul winners were passing out tracts and talking with people on the street when suddenly the girls recognize a familiar face.

"Hey, that was Anton LaVey!" she told her partner. "Hey, Anton, Anton LaVey!" she called out into the crowd. "Yo, Anton, wait up! Anton!" He turned and looked at what he must have known was a spirit-filled Christian.

"Devil, I bind you in the name of Jesus. I bind you and your works..."

The girl shouted and the devil's CEO took off running like a scared jackrabbit. The Christians chased him as far as they could into the crowd, but eventually lost sight of him. Later that evening, when they gave their report back at the church, the entire team got to hear about the exploits of two fearless young believers on a mission from God.

I summed it up by saying, "Hey, gang. Guess what! We got the devil's Most High Unholy Sacrifice last year and this year we've got his chief executive officer on the run!"

A battle was won for the Lord because a handful of seriously committed Christians were passionate about winning lost souls for Jesus. They sought God on their knees and laid prostrate on the church floor in intense prayer for hours because they knew the enemy had it in for them. They knew the enemy was conspiring to destroy them. They fervently called out to God with all their strength, crying tears of compassion because of their desire to see people won to the Lord. And it paid off, big time.

Clearly, people heard from God as He literally directed each and every step of the outreaches. The devil had his goods stolen. Halloweeners came to Christ on the most diabolical anti-Christian holiday of the year, and soul winners witnessed the indisputable, pitiful, impotent condition of the enemy as the devil's true nature was exposed.

It was no wonder my family couldn't come to Fantasy Festivals. I know why God directed me to a water only fast for ten days. We couldn't have accomplished much for God if we had not made ourselves available to God's power and anointing. When we needed it the most, His power was there. God showed up and showed Himself strong on our behalf, and He received all the glory.

≈

## BUSTED FOR HAULING JESUS JUNK

Denny was emotionally, physically, and spiritually drained after doing spiritual warfare with the CEO of the Satanic Church and his followers. I can't imagine a more exhausting week, yet on the way home, Denny had two flat tires and had to have the hearse towed. After the repairs in Miami were completed, he was excited to see his loving family and nobody else. Although he was thoroughly worn out, getting back home to Chicago was the only thing on his mind, so he decided push through and drive all night.

He was traveling outside of Nashville on Interstate 24 when he noticed a bubble in yet another tire. It didn't seem natural to have so many tires go bad, but having no choice in the matter, Denny had to deal with it.

At 7:30 in the morning, rush hour traffic was surging. Vehicles were swarming all around him, so he pulled over onto the shoulder just before an exit ramp and tried to inch his way to the exit. That's when the police car came out of nowhere.

*In his own words...*

"May I see your license and registration, please?"

"Sure thing. Is there a problem, officer? I'm trying to get to a service station before I blow another tire. I just replace two tires down south." I wearily pulled out the receipts from Miami to prove my level of frustration was unfeigned.

"I see," the officer said. "Would you mind pulling up and parking in the grassy area over there?"

"Sure thing, officer. I hope this won't take long. It's been a very long week. I just want to go home."

When I saw several sets of flashing lights on what I assumed were emergency vehicles, I thought there must have been a bad accident somewhere nearby. To my amazement, the emergency vehicles turned out to be the Tennessee SWAT team.

Twelve special agents in full riot gear got out of their vehicles and surrounded the hearse, holding their guns with both hands, their weapons pointed straight up in the air. It looked as if they were standing at attention waiting for their commander to give the signal. I remembered the half circle of paddy wagons in Key

West. The scene seems vaguely familiar, but this incident seemed a bit more curious.

"We'd like permission to search your vehicle," the person in charge said.

"For what?" I asked.

"We have strong reason to believe you might be running drugs or guns."

"Naw, I don't think so," I said. I knew all about vehicle searches and the damage it leaves behind. I remembered what it was like when police stripped my truck in Pennsylvania back when I really was a drug dealer.

"I got a wife and kids I gotta get home to."

"Sir, you should know we will get a search warrant. It'll be here in two or three hours."

"Oh, I see." I thought for a moment. "Well, then, you can search my hearse on one condition. You have to promise to put everything back the way you found it. And, just for your information, so you're not surprised, there's a casket in the back."

"Oh?"

"Oh, yeah. But don't worry. There's no body in it. It's full of Jesus junk."

"Really?"

"Yeah. Really."

They pulled the casket out and unpacked my boxes of Christ in Action tee shirts. Every individual shirt was examined, each collar and seam checked for drugs, every foam JESUS is #1 hand searched. After probing through every inch of every possible space, someone said, "I believe he's telling the truth. This vehicle is filled with a bunch of Jesus junk."

Apparently, the route I was taking from Miami to Chicago was known for drug running, and the haste at which I was traveling (as indicated by the receipts I had shown), indicated the hearse had to be filled with something illegal.

"Listen, can I ask you for one favor? Can I get my camera out and take some pictures? My wife is never going to believe me when I tell her about this."

Busted for transporting Jesus junk, what a legacy! But that's the type of thing that happens when you're a missionary to America on your way back from stealing satan's goods.

# INTO THE NEIGHBORHOODS

"Y ou can't teach what you don't know, and you can't lead where you won't go."

The Christian musician Carmen coined that phrase and the Nissleys lived by it. This credo has taken them into many interesting neighborhoods. Neighborhood is a term used rather loosely here. The Cabrini Green projects in downtown Chicago and South Central Los Angeles are not normally known to be friendly neighborhoods. But that's where Denny and his family ended up so they could help ministers bring the love of Jesus to their communities. Denny has discovered that the most effective approach to reaching spiritually wayward people is to focus on their situation, which means going into their neighborhoods and telling them the truth.

*In his own words...*

"What are you doin' in our 'hood, man? It's after dark," the gang banger declared. "You caint be here, man. The White man don't live long if he stays here after the sun goes down."

"I appreciate the warning, but I'm already in," I said knowing exactly where I was. I was inside the mostly avoided and most feared projects in Chicago.

A bunch of his fellow hoodlums started mouthing off. "What are you, man? KKK?"

I looked around to find out who made that ridiculous statement. "Who said KKK?"

"I did," someone confused.

"I bet you do drugs, don't you?"

"So what if I do?"

"You'd better be on drugs right now to think that I'm that stupid. I might be white, but I ain't stupid. What am I gonna do? You think I'm gonna come into Cabrini Green with two white guys late at night and yell the n-word? You're on drugs, pal. I'm a preacher of the real gospel, and if I can't bring Jesus into your neighborhood, then your neighborhood ain't worth livin' in. Are you listening to me?"

"You a real preacher?" someone else asked.

"Yeah, I'm the real thing."

"Will you pray for my mama? She's real sick. She's bad."

"Yeah, preacher, me, too. If you could just pray for my mama," another person said.

Apparently, kids in gangs have sick mamas and believe in the power of prayer—at least these kids did, and that was good enough for us.

At the time, my buddies and I were in Cabrini Green helping a friend of ours, Dan Taylor, establish a new Christian outreach. At that moment, thirty members of the Disciples street gang heard the requests for prayer. They flocked together to check out what our response would be. They knew we'd have to go into the high-rise apartment building where elevators were commonly used for death chambers. This is where gang members clubbed people to death.

If a gang took us into a dark hallway, we might not see daylight again. Nonetheless, we sensed a secret appreciation and respect toward us for intruding on their turf. We brought with us the possibility of repair for abandoned hopes and forsaken faith.

"Okay, let's go meet mama," I said, swallowing hard.

By the grace of God, the guy with the sick mama lived on the first floor. "You stay outside. I'll bring her to the window," the worried son said.

Mama came to the window looking hopeful. She leaned forward onto the windowsill so we could talk about Jesus. Mama was a believer. It was plain to see her faith in God had sheltered her from the string of tumultuous storms that constantly raged all around her.

"I'm sick, Preacher. Because my son's in a gang."

I tried to be as comforting as I possibly could under the circumstances. I joined hands with her and prayed to God for strength and healing for her mind, soul, and body. Then she joined us as we prayed passionately for the community's recovery.

Immediately, after our collective amens and shots of praise to the Lord, someone else asked, "Hey, man, will you pray for my grandma? Could you ask God to take away her pain? It ain't right, her suffering, an' all."

And the prayer requests came pouring in. We crisscrossed through the middle of the projects in the middle of the night, ministering to the people, and we lived to tell about it.

## HOOD MINISTRY

Before we left, I told the gang about Dan.

"My friend Dan is coming back here to your 'hood. I want you all to welcome him as you did us. He's coming here because he wants to start a Bible study for your 'wannabes.' I'm talking about your little brothers and sisters. You don't want them growing up to be like you, do you?"

The teenagers looked at each other and then hid their eyes from our view. They were unable to look at us. They knew too well they weren't worthy of a blessing but desperately wanted it to happen for their families. The desire of their hearts was to see something good happen for their loved ones. Too many of these kids expected to die violently. They were resigned to such a fate because, in their mind, that was the inescapable destiny life had to offer. To die young was recklessly justified.

It made me sick. It made me weep. It made me want to fight even harder to save souls in Cabrini Green.

"Yeah, Denny. You tell him to come on in. We'll take care of him."

"Good. I expect there won't be any shootin' going on when he's starting up his Bible study. God is God. You treat Him with respect," I told them outright.

"Dat's right, man. We cool with God. Respect."

"That's good to hear. I know if someone killed your buddy, or some stray bullet got a little sister, a lot of you would take justice into your own hands. But we're here to tell you justice has already been taken care of. No one else has to take any more bullets for anyone because Jesus died for all of us. He died of us so we can live free. I admire your loyalty to one another, I really do, but there's something you haven't considered. There's only one Brother who will stick closer to you than anyone in your gang. His name is Jesus, and His power is all the fire power you'll ever need."

That's how we helped start Dan's 'hood ministry—by meeting the needs of the hoodlums. Another Christian ministry was successfully launched in one of American's worst neighborhoods, and as far as I know, no one from God's gang ever got shot.

## WHOSE TURF IS IT REALLY?

Even Hawaii has some pretty tough gangs.

*In his own words...*

I was blessed to have an opportunity to spend six months ministering in Hawaii, and while I was preaching on a street corner in Waikiki, a big Hispanic boy yelled, "Hey! Shut up!"

I saw him and a few of his gang members swarming toward me.

"No, I won't. What's up? Are you from a branch of the Boy Scouts? Girl Scouts, maybe?"

"What did you say? What you don't know, mister, is that I can make one phone call and there will be fifty Bloods here ready, willing, and able to beat you to a pulp!"

"Excuse me? Did you say just one phone call?" I questioned the menacing gang member.

"Yeah, just one."

"Would you? Could you? I'd love to have fifty guys to preach to. Can I give you a quarter? You know how a crowd draws a crowd, so would you go call them as quickly as you can so I can have a crowd to preach to? Please, get them down here, will ya?"

He drew back his arm to lay a monstrous punch on my face, but I caught his fist in the air. I remember thinking, *Look what I snagged. Betcha he's not going to like this.* It was a miracle that made me look powerful, so I took advantage of the moment and started squeezing his fingers.

"Now that I have your attention, let me explain how things really are. You're on my turf. It's my territory because the earth is the Lord's and the fullness thereof, and you're on a street corner with me, so you'd better be nice and polite. If you can't do that, then perhaps you should leave the island as well. Do you understand this?"

"Yes, sir," he said, backing off.

After that day, the Bloods would occasionally hang out a certain distance from my street corner, listening to my messages on the sly. One day, my family and I walked by their favorite street corner, and the Bloods recognized me. At the time, we had five daughters, including Leah, our newborn.

"You that street preacher? Those kids all yours, man? They all your kids?"

"All mine," I replied.

Naturally, I asked them to explain why they call themselves the Bloods, and when it was my turn, I talked about blood as well. I talked about the power in Jesus' blood that covers the sins of the whole world. They listened while I explained the concept of a blood sacrifice. It was something they could relate to, and for many of them it seemed to make sense. The gang bangers were ignorant about the blood of Jesus, so I told them, which is what I think Christ would have done if He had been making friends with the Bloods on a street corner.

~

## GROUND ZERO

But there are more troubled neighborhoods than there are street preachers, Sometimes Christ in Action acts as a stimulus to get churches or other ministries established. Other times, CIA serves as the support system in crisis situations. This was the case in 1990 when Denny and his family traveled to South Central Los Angeles to help a church called Victory Outreach.

He parked his MCI motorcoach bus on a nice concrete slab that may have previously been a nice building. The building had burned down in the riots after the Rodney King verdicts were announced. Although it had been years since the riots, it was pretty obvious the bus was parked in a war zone. Racial tension permeated the air, so Victory Outreach posted a security guard outside the bus 24 hours a day so no one could damage it or try to steal it. Even though the community had made attempts to reduce crime, the citizens hadn't entirely given up their appetite for violence.

Victory Outreach wanted to offer the community healing through an impressive one-day street party and festival following a week of outreach. They blocked off three blocks and seven lanes of traffic at Manchester and Broadway, the exact epicenter of the riots.

They set up a stage with a backdrop and a powerful sound system with tower speakers. Musicians attracted crowds with contemporary Christian music. They had plenty of good food and a steady stream of people all day. Then, at dusk, the Victory Outreach actors and actresses filtered themselves out of the crowd and into position for the performance of the drama.

*In his own words...*

An officer of the law arrived on the scene.

"Listen, officer, we want to let you in on a secret. We're getting ready to put on a drama that's seriously realistic. It's called *Straight from the 'Hood*, but the guns and blood aren't real. It's all Hollywood. We're going to scare some folks tonight, but we don't want it to be you."

"Good idea. I'm sure glad you warned us."

"We're hoping to scare people right outta hell into heaven," I told him.

"May I suggest you double-check your props? We wouldn't want any accidents to happen out here tonight." The suggestion was received, and every prop was double-checked.

After watching the forty-five-minute drama, about a thousand people gave their lives to the Lord that night at the altar call. Christians ministered one-on-one to victims of violent crimes. The pastor had an altar call specifically for victims of violent crimes and six to eight hundred people flooded the front area. Then he made another announcement and something remarkable happened.

"If anyone has bigotry in their heart, pray and let God heal you. Let Him forgive you and then go find a member of another race and give him or her a hug," the pastor said to the crowd.

"Say something like, 'I forgive you' and hug their neck til God says let go. Would you let God have His way tonight? Don't be stubborn. God is not pleased with the rebellion that has taken place here, but He stands ready to restore you and this community because He is the God of love and restoration. Let's get rid of the hate, shall we?"

People started to openly hug people. It was not what the police and the community expected would take place at our post-riot rally. I had a line a block long because I was the only white man in the area at the time. I thought, *Am I ever going to see the end of this line? And Lord, they're all waiting in line because until today they used to have a problem with hatred—towards me! What if someone's not completely healed?* I stood out in the crowd, and in fact, during the weeks my family and I had been in Los Angeles, we were the only white people in the area for days.

As I embraced one person after another, I felt the presence of God dissolving an assortment of hardheartedness, and I started to cry. One black man hugged me and turned to walk away, but I grabbed him by his jacket and said, "You didn't give it up, did you? You still hate me, don't you? You don't like the white man, do you? I know where you're at because I used to be a bigot. I used to hate people just because they were black. If you'd just release it to God and give it up, God will set you free to love all people. Trust me, it's true."

He looked at me for a good while, and when the wall of hate fell, we held each other and wept, right there in South Central LA, right there, where years before people had killed people just because of the color of their skin.

I found my wife later and asked her, "Sandy, did you see what happened when the pastor dealt with hatred between the races?"

"I sure did!"

"Did people form a line to hug on you and the kids? They did with me. For over an hour, I was a white hugging post!"

The police said they had never had that many people in one place at one time before. They wouldn't have allowed it. The potential for trouble was unthinkable. But God showed up in the 'hood, and there was not one arrest, distress call, or major problem.

# A REASON TO PREACH

Denny never knows who will be affected by his preaching or how far God will take him into the kingdom of darkness to be a beacon of His glorious light, but since he's been willing to preach for little or no reason, the results have been blessed.

In this case, all it took was an ugly necktie. This necktie was black with the names of famous streets displayed all over it in bright colors—Rodeo Drive, Wall Street, Park Avenue, Bourbon Street, and so on. One of Denny's many friends thought a street preacher ought to have a "street" necktie. Although Denny says it was the devil who invented the necktie, God used this particular necktie for good.

*In his own words...*

At one point in my ministry, I realized I had preached on nearly all of the streets on my tie except for Abbey Road in London, England, and thus I developed a desire to preach on Abbey Road. I eventually ended up in London, found Abbey Road, and discovered that the famous street is in a residential neighborhood. The street, by the way, is lined with row homes, except for Abbey Road Studios made famous by the Beatles and one high-rise apartment building.

There I was, so there I preached.

I looked around at all the people not there. There was no one to preach to except a few playful squirrels. Just so I could say I did it, I decided to preach anyway. I asked myself, *What exactly does one preach when no one's listening?* I used my imagination and envisioned hundreds of people and lifted my voice for about twenty minutes, proclaiming the plan of salvation while my friends Martin and Daryn walked around looking for someone to hand a gospel tract to.

I thought, *This is brutal. What a waste of time. Not a soul in sight. The squirrels must think I'm the one nut they'll never crack.* And then, a few minutes into the experiment, I felt a special anointing from God and I knew God wanted me there. I told myself someone must be listening or I wouldn't have felt the presence of God. When the anointing lifted, I stopped and looked around. Things did not look promising. Then I saw Martin talking with one exceptionally animated guy across the street.

"Brother Denny! Come here," Martin shouted. "Meet the Sheik!"

"Hi, I'm Denny."

"You are fundamentalist, no?" Not waiting for my reply, the Sheik continued. "I said to myself I must go meet this radical fundamentalist who preaches when there's no one to listen, yet I hear his words through my closed window. I am fundamentalist Muslim. I am pleased to meet my brother."

"Ah, Sheik, I'm glad you came out and all, but I am not your brother. To be brothers, you and I would have to have the same Dad. God is my Father."

"God is my father, too!" he protested, then spat on the ground in disgust.

"Not the God of the Bible," I insisted.

"God of Quran!"

"See? What did I tell you? Different."

The sheik started to shake. "You Americans. I dislike you Americans."

He spat again. For about an hour, we discussed religions and world events. I found out this man was one of the most influential Muslims of the time. Ironically, he was raised by Catholic nuns in Mexico City, educated in the United States, and received his Ph.D. in Berkeley, California, yet he hated Americans.

"What do you think of Louis Farrakhan?" I asked.

He spat. "Louis Farrakhan is not fundamentalist!"

"I agree with you, but don't spit. What do you think about Libya's Muammar al-Gaddafi?"

"He is not a true fundamentalist," he said after spitting one more time for emphasis.

He went on to explain fundamentalism in general and Islamic faith in particular. The conversation was intriguing. I'll never forget what he told me. According to this man, Muslims believe that a thief probably won't change; therefore, when a Muslim kills a thief, he is stealing the thief's soul from the devil, and the soul goes to heaven. But if a thief happens to die in a car accident,

Muslims believe the thief's soul will go to hell. When fundamentalist Muslims kill people, they truly believe they're working for God.

Only the truth could set them free from this murderous lie. As I listened, I waited for an opening in the conversation.

"Muslims can't marry a woman unless her father is a keeper of the book," Sheik informed us.

"What book?"

"The Quran, the Bible, or the Torah, any of those three."

"So, you read the Bible," I said. My moment had arrived. "Who is Jesus to you?" I asked.

"Jesus was a prophet, a good prophet."

"Well, I have to tell you Jesus said, 'I am the Way, the Truth, and the Life. No one comes to the Father except through me.' And if Jesus is the prophet you say He is, then that pretty much cuts out Allah, and Mohammed is toast."

"I don't like you Americans! If you speak against the Quran, we will kill you. You will die! I know you speak out of ignorance, or I should kill you here and now!"

"Well, I'd have to say you know don't me very well because I speak against it quite often."

He was furious yet curious about what or who made me so bold. We talked at length about what he thought should be done in Jerusalem. I, of course, told him what the Bible says about Jerusalem. Despite our differences, he liked me well enough to invite me to attend his family's mosque in Lebanon if I ever found myself looking for a famous street corner in his country.

"I have never heard Christianity explained this way in all my life," he admitted before we parted company.

I was amazed but not surprised. It was because of an ugly tie that this ardent Muslim leader stopped long enough to talk to a street preacher about Jesus and examine Christianity from a new perspective.

# HANG HIM FROM HIS OWN CROSS

I t's always a temptation for a street preacher like Denny to preach when a crowd is gathered. His large stature and booming voice commands people's attention from the get-go. He cannot go unnoticed in a crowd. Give him a ten-foot wooden cross and put him in a rally with a million black men, and he will garner attention. And it probably won't be the good kind. Nonetheless, Denny knew God wanted him to proclaim the gospel message at the Million Man March in Washington, D.C. in October 1996.

He wasn't deterred by the multiple messages he received that his very life was in danger as a white Christian preacher in a black man's rally. Preaching to this particular crowd proved to be just that...life threatening, which is why Denny was not surprised when an angry mob searched for a rope to hang him from his own cross.

God had a different plan in mind.

*In his own words...*

Looking back, it's within the realm of divine possibility that the real reason a million black men came together was to hear the gospel, but as I chopped firewood on the Saturday morning before the march, I wrestled with a desire to preach there. *Do you want me to go, Lord? I want to be sure you want me there.* I received my answer. *Go to the Million Man March and preach, but I want you to know the enemy has an assignment for your life.*

I turned off the chainsaw, *Am I going to die?* This I said out loud.

Silence. *Am I going to live?* Nothing.

All I knew was that God wanted me to go to the rally and the enemy was going to try to take my life when I got there. Now my problem became how to inform Sandy...*Hi, honey. It's Saturday. I might be dying Monday.* I told her I was going but kept my concerns in my heart and continued to pray.

## SUNDAY MORNING

During the announcements at our Sunday morning service at Manassas Assembly of God, my pastor, Charles Nestor, declared to the thousand or more churchgoers that I was going to the Million Man March.

"Let's remember to keep Denny in our prayers."

There was concern on his part. Apparently, my going to the march was a big deal.

Immediately after the service, a distinct trend began to take place. I will always obey the prompting of the Holy Spirit to go somewhere to proclaim the Good News, but it's highly irregular for the Holy Spirit to tell other people that I might die doing it.

A woman found me in the lobby and said, "God told me to pray for you while you're at the march." She paused. "Brother Denny, God told me to pray for your life."

I locked eyes with her somewhat surprised. "Then, girlfriend, I suggest you pray!"

From the foyer, a brother backed me into a corner to say, "About that rally. I'll be praying for you. God told me to pray for your life, Reverend."

"I really hope you're obedient, brother."

Hmmmm. When the same thing happened in the parking lot, I concluded people were on to something. These independent confirmations validated my word from God. I continued to pray and also decided I would need to find some time to get my affairs in order before Monday morning.


SUNDAY AFTERNOON

Someone from the church's outreach ministries had obtained a permit for that Sunday afternoon to preach on the steps of the Capitol building, the precise location of Minister Farrakhan's impending address. A few church members and I took a handheld public address system so we could proclaim holy ground and make a stand for truth at that historic site. There were hundreds of black men hanging around waiting for the main event scheduled to begin in less than twenty-four hours.

After singing a round of praise and worship songs, the Christians began preaching over the public address system. We came face-to-face with an entourage of Nation of Islam men whose demeanor seemed to suggest, *Touch me and you will die.*

"Hey, how come you're protesting?" one man spoke out loud.

"I ain't protesting nothing. I'm proclaiming," I said nonchalantly. "There's a big difference."

"What are you proclaiming?" asked a man in a bow tie. He appeared to be an authority of some kind.

"Salvation through Jesus Christ and Him alone," I answered. "I'm proclaiming liberty in Christ."

A conversation about doctrine followed, and I share the plan of salvation with him. Since the gospel can't be preached openly in Islamic societies, many Muslims have never heard the Good News, met a true Christian, or seen a Bible. Some face certain death if they convert to Christianity.

Nevertheless, I couldn't stay away when the outspoken leader of the Nation of Islam Louis Farrakhan opened a spiritual umbrella under the guise of a sacred assembly, touting atonement for all in hopes of persuading more black people to commit to his cause. However, the wind of truth began to blow through Farrakhan's assembly when some prayed-up soul winners showed up with their weatherworn Bibles, a small public address system, and a crazy street preacher with a ten-foot wooden cross.

## A DIVINE APPOINTMENT

"Do you know who that was?" someone in our group asked after the man in authority left.

"Yeah, a Muslim," I replied.

"Yeah, a Muslim by the name of Dr. Abdul Alim Muhammed."

"Oh. Dr. Who, now?"

"Abdul Alim Muhammed, Minister Ali. He's Louis Farrakhan's right-hand man for this march and one of the highest-ranking men in the Nation of Islam. Everything goes by him."

"Still a sinner," I said.

The Christians returned to their assignment of worshipping the Lord. Forty-five minutes later, a motorcade of Nation of Islam vehicles stopped in front of the team, and Minister Alim confidently approached.

I could hardly contain my delight.

"Hey, you're back! You want to repent and become a Christian, right?"

"No."

"What are you wasting my time then?" I asked in an overly sweet tone.

Minister Alim let out a muffled laugh and admitted, "I like you."

I immediately asked him to write his name and phone number on a 3" x 5" index card, and then I handed him my business card. "This is your lucky day. I'm gonna let you buy me lunch sometime," I said. And then I added, "I eat a lot."

"I like you," he said again.

"You said that twice."

"I like that cross."

"It's all right. The original one was better."

"I would like this cross to be in my March tomorrow."

"Well, it's my cross."

"I would like you to carry it."

I was dumbfounded.

## SUNDAY EVENING

Our group returned to Manassas later that night to attend the Sunday evening service. Pastor Nestor once again announced his desire for people to pray for me. Out of the blue, he asked me to come forward so the elders and the staff could lay hands on me and pray.

I thought, *This is getting intense. He's never called me up front before.* The prayer focused on my physical safety and included a plea to spare my life. There it was again. Something was definitely brewing.

Before leaving the church, a black brother told me he wanted to go along to the march. I thought it would be good to have a black man with me at a black man's rally. I invited him to come home with me that night to sleep on our couch so we could get an early start. I planned to leave at 4:30 in the morning in order to find a decent place to park.

As Sandy and I got ready for bed, I decided it was time to confront my wife with the seriousness of the situation, "You know it can get pretty, ah, intense tomorrow."

She turned around from where she was standing and stared at me. "I know. You know you could die tomorrow," she said.

I thought about that for a moment and said, "Yeah, well, I could die any day on the freeway. Why'd you say that?"

"I didn't want to tell you, but, ah, I was praying, and the Lord told me you were going to go, and He also told me you might die."

"Wow! Guess what God told me while I was chopping wood on Saturday. Why didn't you tell me?"

"I didn't want to worry you. Why didn't you tell me?" she asked, already knowing the answer. My wife, the mother of our seven daughters, expecting our eighth child, knew the answer. Apparently, no one needed to worry. Everyone needed to pray.

I told Sandy I was willing to go to the Million Man March if that's what the Lord wanted. We both had faith to believe that God was able to deliver, that was never the question. The fact was God's plan might not include deliverance, and it had to be said out loud.

"God is able to deliver, but there's a chance He might not. So, there's no problem. I'm going?"

She nodded.

"Since we don't have a problem with me going, there are some things I'd like to tell you."

We stayed up until after two o'clock in the morning getting our affairs in order.

"I have a will prepared. Call the board members. They'll all come. God will supply for you and the girls."

The tedious task ended with a discussion of our life insurance plan. When we felt we had covered all the details, Sandy asked, "Do we wake up the girls?"

"No. I don't want to worry them."

The hardest part was telling my wife what to tell the girls.

"Tell them I'm not afraid of dying. Tell Rachel...Tell Bethany... Tell Melody...Tell Deborah...Tell Elizabeth...Tell Leah...Tell Grace..." The emotional exhaustion of it all came crashing in. I took a quick shower and fell into bed.

Two hours later, I got ready to leave, stepped outside my bedroom, and saw my second oldest daughter Bethany. "Hi, Dad!"

I thought, *Bethany, do you always hang out here at 4:30 in the morning?*

"Just wanted to say good-bye one more time, Dad."

I tried to hold back tears. "Bye, sweetheart." I hugged my daughter for what I hoped would not be the last time. I found out later that Bethany, who was eleven at the time, went into her bedroom and prayed form 4:30 to 5:30 that morning.


## MONDAY MORNING

The outreach team had gone to DC on Sunday, but there were just two of us going for the actual march. When my lone companion and I arrived at Union Station with the ten-foot cross, we were immediately barraged with media.

"Who are you? Why are you here?" they asked us.

I answered the question by starting to preach, saying, "I'm here to share Christ."

Someone yelled out, "Hey! This isn't a religious thing. It's a black thing!"

I looked out at some angry faces and shouted as loud as I could. "No, that's where you're wrong. This isn't a skin thing. It's a sin thing!"

It became the theme song for the day. My friend and I continued walking toward the Capitol. "You're the craziest man in the universe!" my companion exclaimed.

I quickly assessed my helper. He was a hard-core, beat 'em up, shoot 'em up, former gang banger from the West Coast. Both parents had been killed in driveway shootings. He had been in and out of jail since was he was fifteen years old. He was a real tough guy, but even he wasn't comfortable in our situation.

Unless I called him over to where I was standing, he stayed a safe distance from me. I never felt more alone with Jesus in all my life.

We walked on and set up the cross alongside the Capitol building. When I started preaching, it was 8:00 AM. March attendees gathered around. Some seemed enraged by my preaching and proclaimed their intentions.

"Let's hang him. That's what they did to our forefathers!" a couple of leader-types yelled. Several other men started combing the area for a rope. "Yeah, let's hang him from his own cross!"

I found out later, back at the Nissley home, at 7:30 in the morning, Bethany woke up her older sister Rachel.

"What are you doing?" Rachel asked.

"We need to pray for Daddy," Bethany insisted.

They prayed for an hour the morning of the march. Evidently, my life depended on God and the prayers of godly children and obedient saints.

As the mob got more riled, I considered the likelihood that Daniel might have had the opportunity to guess which lion would be the first to grab him for lunch. *Which angry man will throw the first punch? Will my wife and children see my name in tomorrow's newspapers? Will I make front page news? Could this be the event that sends this street preacher home to be with Jesus?*

I asked God, *What do you want me to say? What can I say that won't arouse their wrath?* Someone in the crowd wanted to know what color Jesus was. Another person was concerned about specific doctrinal issues.

A voice cried out, "Was it Ishmael on Abraham's altar? I believe it was Ishmael on that altar!"

"Wow," I exclaimed. I was amazed but not dazed. Quiet inspiration came to my rescue.

"You must be a theologian. I'm just a dumb street preacher. You know what? You might be right, but answer this question, who was the ram in the thicket? Who was the sacrifice that God gave in place of Abrahams's son? You see, I'm here today to tell you, a million of you, that it was Jesus who was sacrificed. Today, it should be your behind and mine on the altar, but we can't pay enough to cover our sins. The substitute ram was Jesus, and He died for the blacks, the whites, the Asians, and the Hispanics. He died for all of us! Let's say Ishmael was on that altar if you like it better that way. That's fine with me, but answer this question, will you bow down to Jesus? Will you put Jesus where He belongs? Will you...?"

That was not the sermon they came to hear. A guy in a crisp bow tie came face-to-face, nose-to-nose with me and proceeded to shout, "Shut up! Shut up or I'm going to knock your head off!"

"What's your name?"

"My name's Brian," he said, spitting. "I don't hang with white trash."

"Okay, Brian. I'm going to let you in on a secret."

The disturbance was growing and drawing attention when two police officers suddenly came out of nowhere. "Is there a problem here, gentlemen?"

They looked at the two of us, trying to size up the situation.

"No, sir, no problem here. Brian and I were just talking."

Immediately after the officers left, I made sure Brian knew I was there at the Million Man March as the invited guest of Dr. Abdul

Alim Muhammad. I showed him the index card with Minister Alim's name and phone number.

"Remember, Brian, it's the Day of Atonement. Everyone's welcome. And, for your information, Minister Alim and I are going to have lunch together. You see, Brian, Minister Alim is interested in my cross. And there's something else you should know. Evidently, he's not consumed with hate and vengeance, and he's certainly not interested in hanging me from my own cross."

Brian finally left in a huff and melted back into the crowd.

The crowd's intensity, however, did not diminish when Brian left. But, about ten minutes later, I saw a sight that made me stop and stare. In all my life, I had never seen a more beautiful thing. The white, hand-painted sign with blood red letters read: JESUS SAVES—ONLY HE DELIVERS.

I saw a black arm holding the sign, but he was an ocean away. Keeping my eyes fixed on the sign, I realized it wouldn't be long before the sign carrier would see my ten-foot cross in the sea of humanity. Eventually, our eyes met, and after several prolonged moments, we found each other within the thickening crowd.

"I love you, brother!" the man shouted as he let his sign drop to the ground.

We hugged one another joyfully, both of us thrilled to find an ally amidst the crowd. Since I wasn't expecting any support, when I saw a fellow Christian come out from the multitude, I figured I was looking at an angel.

## THIS ANGEL CAN PREACH!

That angel was named Warren. He fearlessly took on the adversary, fully engaged in the battle for men's souls.

"Who can deliver you, black man? Muhammad? Allah? They cannot. Bring me the man who can deliver you. Is it Farrakhan? I tell you the truth. Farrakhan cannot deliver you." Warren began fervently preaching some radical material. He paused only to look at me long enough to ask, "Am I doing all right? I've never done street preaching before."

"All right?!" Grateful for this unexpected help and astonished by this brother's boldness on his first day on the job, I quickly added, "Brother, you keep it up! You're not bad for a rookie!"

But venom, hate, and murder oozed from the eyes all around us. Why did all the angry guys seem to show up at our location? When the crowd's collective pent-up aggression looked as though it was aimed for a deadly assault on Warren, I started preaching to shift their animosity to another target—me. Warren started back up again the minute the attack got too heavy for me. Like a tag team, the two preachers kept going for over an hour until a determined committee decided to put an end to it. The Muslims extended a personal challenge to their brother, Warren.

"Brother," their leader said. "Why don't you join your black family? We've put on the biggest family reunion ever. The whole family's here. Why don't you leave this ugly piece of white trash, fat garbage and join your family?"

Warren looked at me, then at the crowd. He looked at them individually while they anxiously waited for his response. Then, Warren locked eyes with the leader of the pack.

"Family, is not about the color of your skin!" He had their attention.

"You don't get it, do you? Family means you have the same Father. This piece of white trash and I have the same Father. Our Father has an only son, who happens to be the heir to everything Father has, and we've been adopted into Father's family. Only thing is, because of our sins, the son had to die in order for us to get in. We're brothers because of the sacrifice of Father's son. The son's name is Jesus, and Father raised Him from the dead—took Him right out of the grave, overcoming death and defeating hell itself. Our Father promised we would do the same if we accept His son, Jesus, whom He sent because He loves us."

Warren concluded his passionate speech with the following.

"Listen to me. It's our Father who will one day say to Louis Farrakhan, 'Go to hell, I don't know you.' This is what will happen to your leader if he doesn't repent before God for his sins."

They did not like hearing this. I thought, *Dude, you're gonna get us killed. But hey, at least I'm going to heaven with an angel!* It had occurred to me that I might die that day, but I never thought I'd be departing with an angel named Warren.

Feeling restored, I added, "Will our Father look at you and tell you "Go to hell' because He doesn't know you either?

With that, we were done. Warren left, and the young man from my church and I headed back to the van.

MONDAY EVENING

I couldn't wait to rejoin my family. We met at a sandwich shop. I was overcome with emotion when I saw them. I hugged my wife and children, drinking in their love. It was as if I was absorbing everything I possibly could from them.

"Daddy! Daddy's home!"

"Dad," Rachel said, getting ready to unburden herself.

"I am so glad to see you! I prayed for you, Dad. God had me pray for your life. I just felt as if the devil would try to take your life. Tell us, Dad. What happened?"

Denny told his oldest daughter, with tears in his eyes, all that took place, pointing out that if he had a dollar for every time someone threatened his life, he could pay off their mortgage. In addition, he told her that if he had a dollar for every time someone asked him what color skin Jesus had, they could eat really well for at least a year. He told them that each time he tried to inject the salvation message into the Million Man March, someone in the crowd went into a frenzy.

But Denny lived to talk about it. The enemy never likes it when a Christian, especially a bold street preacher, invades his turf, but God loves it. In fact, God may very well have sent an angel to prove it.

# MARDI GRAS, HOSTILE TERRITORY

Mardi Gras officially begins on January 6, the Feast of the Epiphany, which honors the day the three kings visited the Christ child. Mardi Gras ends with Fat Tuesday, the day before Ash Wednesday, which is the beginning of Lent. Revelers come to New Orleans from all over the world to make sure they have something to repent for during Lent. It's the ultimate Party-Now, Pay-Later plan. The celebration sanctions sin and promotes promiscuity, the likes of which, some say, has not been seen since the days of Sodom and Gomorrah. For this reason, New Orleans during Mardi Gras is hostile territory for church folk.

This chapter is a medley of Mardi Gras experiences spanning a number of years. Since establishing his ministry, Denny has challenged people to reach out beyond what's comfortable so they can grow in their walk with the Lord. It's one of the most extreme growth opportunities a Christian can have. It has a life-changing effect on both Christians and non-Christians. I know. I've been there.

The kind of ministry that takes place during Mardi Gras has a flavor all its own. Anywhere else, it would completely outrageous, but in New Orleans at Mardi Gras, anything goes. One year, a pastor from South Carolina decided to experience the outreach for himself. He came up with an unusual method of getting people to listen.

"I have to have your attention," the pastor turned street preacher said.

"Yes, you! Everyone up on that balcony. I need you to listen to what I'm getting ready to say. Give me your attention, please. I must have your attention," he declared matter-of-factly.

"I'm going to UNZIP...my coat...ALL THE WAY!"

Without exception, every head on the balcony turned to see whatever it was he was going to expose, their flesh so addicted to sin, they couldn't help themselves. The befuddled crowd heard the unzipping of a rookie street preacher's mouth.

"God loves you! No matter who you are. No matter what you've done. You don't need to drown your sorrows with alcohol. Jesus can fill you with Living Water so you will never thirst again!"

That's one example of how the gospel is preached Bourbon Street. Thanks to Christ in Action ministries, men and women of God gather from all over so they have conversations with the inebriated partygoers on the streets during Mardi Gras. Since Denny can't preach salvation to all of America himself, he set his face like a flint to set ablaze people's passion for winning lost souls for Christ. The streets of New Orleans are swarming with needy people, which makes the soul winner wonder, *Which one, Lord? Which poor soul do you want to reach through me?*

Soul winners must be ready to do spiritual warfare, which includes prayer and fasting before every outreach event. Once on site, they're required to follow the schedule and rules explicitly. If they don't, they're sent home at their own expense. Each day begins with mandatory quiet time, Bible reading, and prayer, followed by an hour or more of praise and worship and a time of exhortation and teaching. It's vitally important that the troops prepare themselves spiritually before they go into battle.

The devil doesn't like it when Christians go directly into his territory to retrieve lost souls. Christians who want to experience divine appointments must first acquire a divine anointing by denying their flesh, which is why Denny never dispatches anyone onto the streets thinking they're fueled up on their own strength. They must empty themselves so they can be filled with the Holy Spirit. If they're willing to do that, then Denny can be assured they will do serious damage out there on what used to be the devil's turf.

## VAGABOND REBEL TEENS

While there seems to be an inexhaustible supply of needy people on the streets of New Orleans, none were more despised than the gutter punks, whose world, at the time, was especially dark. The city supported approximately five hundred or so gutter punk kids at the peak of Mardi Gras, though probably thousands were migrating all over the country. New Orleans had what they needed—abandoned buildings, dumpsters, a Bohemian party atmosphere, and plenty of half-filled cups of beer and booze to pick up off curbs or scarfed from trash cans and tabletops.

In the middle of Mardi Gras 1996, the people of New Orleans made it their mission to run the gutter punks out of town. When Denny heard that, he knew it was time to once again to take the love of Jesus to where's its most desperately needed and hardest to find. This time, it would be to the social outcasts recognized for their lawlessness and grunge.

Because the punks scared the tourists, they were being arrested for crimes such as "impersonating a human being" and petty things such as "blocking a public walkway." The merchants, fed up with their panhandling, public urination, drunkenness, and fighting circulated posters picturing the gutter punks and stated: DON'T FEED THE ANIMALS!

To the soul winners, the punks looked like a cross between the hobos of the '20 and '30s and the hippies of the '60s. Although some thought they acted like animals without souls, God showed Denny's crew of soul winners that they were made in His image, and it was for them Christ died. They had no defenders, that is until some spirit-filled Christians showed up with a message from Calvary.

People who live on the streets have the basis desire to belong to a loving family. The gutter punk kids were convinced they had found the family they had always wanted and needed in each other. The year 1996 became the year of ministry to the gutter punks as CIA teams encountered the transient teens throughout Mardi Gras. One team reported how they were able to reach a small group of wayward teens.

"They don't like being called gutter punks," Jerry told his partner Linda.

"Yes, they do," Linda said. "They'll tell you, that's who they are. I gave a balloon sculpture to three of them earlier and they seemed genuinely touched."

Linda went on to describe the scruffy looking girls. One girl outfitted herself in what appeared to be a deteriorating quilt. Pieces of outdated garments, most of which were frayed and soiled, had been sewn together randomly so as to create a long, warm, winter garment.

"Bet you thought we would hurt you," one girl blurted out.

"No," Linda said. "Why would I think that? I don't know anything about you. Who are you?"

"I'm Sky This is Eyelet. This is Patches. I thought maybe you heard about us from the TV. They've said we beat up tourists and stuff."

"My name is Linda, and this is Jerry. All I know is that you live on the streets because you choose to. I suppose you're making a statement, or something. I'm not sure."

"A statement? You think I'm here by choice? If I had a place, I'd be in it right now watching Ricki Lake or The People's Court with Judge what's-his-face.

"Oh, I see. I guess it would be fair to say that aside from your housing arrangements, you're living what you believe? Kinda like what Jerry and I are doing."

"Living what you believe," Eyelet repeated the phrase thoughtfully. "Yeah, that's cool."

Linda shared her testimony with Sky, Eyelet, and Patches. The girls, drawn into Linda's story, spent twenty minutes absorbed in the highlights of Linda's ravaged then redeemed life. Jerry had quietly planted himself in the background and prayed God would save their souls and keep them safe from harm.

Linda listened as they opened up and shared their beliefs. Never once did she whip out her Bible and point her finger in condemnation. She spoke the truth in love. It ended with a group hug. Both team members understood that it was up to the Holy Spirit to convince, convict, and comfort the young women.

"Listen. You girls take care of yourselves." Linda found it hard to let them go. "It's a very dangerous world out there.

Denny had instructed the soul winners to love on the kids first. Linda had listened. She concentrated on connecting with the kids to establish a relationship with them so that maybe someday it would pay off. Obviously, the gutter punk kids had some off the wall, messed-up values, but to a discerning heart willing to look closer, it became apparent that these kids aligned themselves with people who care and that they valued relationships.

"We're feeding your tribe tonight at the Wall. Tell all your friends," Linda added. "Tell 'em we'll have vegetarian stew and plenty of dog biscuits."

The Wall, located at the end of Elysian Fields Avenue, is where a wall separates the French Quarter from the Mississippi River.

"Wow! That's cool. People don't do stuff like that for us. We'll be there!"

The girls sauntered off into the crowd.

## EXTREME EVANGELISM

Actually, Christ in Action brought more than dog biscuits and stew. We had 80 gallons of hot chocolate, 700 cans of soda, mega coolers full of hot vegetarian stew, 1,000 hamburgers, and some packaged condiments. The Wall became an outdoor restaurant for the homeless. We also had a van full of clothing, three hundred wool blankets, and hundreds of pairs of new cotton tube socks to give away.

"Hey, preacher!" someone yelled out. "Someone told us you brought dog biscuits. We want to feed our dogs before we eat."

"That's too bad," Denny answered. "We're feeding you first."

"Then we won't eat!" the rebel replied.

"That's fine with me. Jesus died for people, not dogs. You're more important to Jesus than the dogs are. Because you don't know God, your priorities are out of whack. But hey, if you insist, my crew will pack up the food…"

"Wait! Uh, no, don't do that, and. You promise to feed the dogs?"

"Yes, as soon as we're done feeding you. Listen, I came here from Washington DC. These people helping me came from all over the United States of America. We heard the police were trying to run you out of town. We want you to realize that we're here because we give a rip about your lives. The police don't love you. They don't even like you. They want you gone."

And since Denny knew they hated most Christians, he said, using his best preaching voice, "And, oh, by the way. We're Christians. We want to feed you because we love you. We want to be a part of your family tonight. I know some of you think we hate you, but you're wrong. We love you. Look around. There are hundreds of Christians here lovin' on you! We took time off from our jobs without pay to be here. We left family behind to be here because we heard about your plight. We were concerned when we heard about your situation on TV. Now, let's thank God for the grub."

After Denny's speech, they were respectful and even polite. I'm sure people were surprised when many bowed their heads for prayer. Then, one by one, they cheerfully came through the food line, and they showed how much they cared about each other while doing it.

"No thanks, man. I already had some. I don't need it, but my friend, he does. Can I have this for my friend over there?" one boy said, pointing to a slumped over kid.

The punks sat in groups of six or eight along with one or two of us Christians. We had sweet fellowship with the angry young rebels as well as a few homeless adults. Amazingly, after a short while, the bone through the nose didn't matter. The colored spiked hair and the hateful tattoos became pretty much invisible. The outreach was such a success, Denny decided to do it again on Monday night. He announced his intentions over the microphone, including how to get a free blanket and some socks.

Monday night it rained, so we covered ourselves with plastic trash bags and fed them again. I overheard one kids telling a soul winner, "Hey, remember me from the other night? You said if I found you here tonight, you'd give me a blanket."

"We ran out of blankets, but I saved one for you. It's behind the seat of our truck. Wait here. I'll go get it," he said.

"Thanks, man," the kid said. "I really effing appreciate this. Now I can sleep." He paused. "Ya know, ain't nobody ever stood out in the rain with us. Ever!"

We hadn't planned on such a strange outreach, but God must have because we were reaching people from all walks of life. Denny's mother, along with most of the CIA kitchen crew, came Monday night to witness firsthand the unusual ministry. Through an open window in the back of one of the CIA vans, Denny's mom overheard a conversation she'll never forget.

"Do you know what kind of Christians these are?" a guy asked his friend.

"They're religious, but ya know what I think? I think this is what Christians should be doing."

"I don't know, man. I can't figure it out, but I agree. And they're not shouting at us."

We did give them the message, though.

## TESTIMONY TIME

There's nothing more exciting for an evangelist than leading someone to the Lord. Denny loves to reel them into the kingdom of God, especially when he pulls them out of the devil's sea of despair. He's overjoyed when he gets to be a part of someone's salvation experience, but the greatest part of his outreach ministry comes during testimony time when he gets to hear ordinary Christians tell their extraordinary stories of God's love and grace.

Some soul winners can't get a good night's rest until they've shared their victory stories, so each night Denny lets them share their experiences, no matter how late or exhausted the group might be. Not everyone hits a home run every time at bat, so testimony time also provided much needed encouragement for those who may have struck out.

Just outside of the city, at the host church, it was two o'clock in the morning when Martin couldn't wait to share his story.

"I felt as if the Lord was telling me to just talk. I believe He was showing me that because of my British accent, people would listen to what I had to say. So that's what I did, Brother Denny. I chatted all night long, and now my voice is completely gone, glory to God!" reported the banker by trade, soul winner by grace.

"I want you all to know," Denny said after the laughter subsided, "Martin's from London. He's here on holiday. That's British for vacation, y'all. Martin, are you having a good holiday?" Denny asked in his best British accent.

"You know I aa-ammmm, my bra-tha," Martin replied in his best southern accent.

"Anyone else?" Denny asked the ragged group. A young man stood up.

"Brothers and sisters, I don't know if you noticed it or not, but there are a lot of backslidden Christians out there. One of them urinated on the cross when we were preaching on Bourbon Street. But as soon as he zipped up his pants, the power of God hit him so hard he fell to the ground, sobbing like a baby. So, I grabbed Brian and Dave and went to him. We knelt down beside him, put our arms around him, and prayed with him, right there in the middle of the street. It was at the foot of our peed-on cross that the backslidden Sunday school teacher rededicated his life to the Lord."

Even though, prior to testimony time, any measure of physical strength we might have had left was nearly extinguished from laboring on the streets all day and night, the saints celebrated God's mercy with renewed fervor.

"But that's not all, Brother Denny. When we got up from our knees and took him off to the side, he was completely sober. He knew exactly what he was doin'. We took him to a pay phone so he could call a cab. He wanted nothin' to do with Mardi Gras! Isn't God good, y'all?"

The happy hollering went on until Denny told the exhausted group, "Get outta here, you bunch of fanatics. You Jesus lovers, you! Ten minutes til lights out."

"Vait, Brother Denny! You must tell dem about us!" someone called out in a heavy Russian accent.

"Oh, yeah. Folks, hang on a minute. You won't believe this. We happened to have with us two Russian evangelists from Pennsylvania. It was their turn to go the microphone and read the Bible."

Each year at Mardi Gras, teams from Christ in Action read through the Bible in its entirety in Jackson Square. We set up a booth next to the soothsayers and fortunetellers to read God's Word aloud and to pass out New Testaments to people.

"I asked them to read in their native language and guess who just happened to be in the crowd at that time? Two Russian businessmen. When they heard their native language being spoken over our puny sound system, they rushed over to see what was going on. They had never heard the Word of God before, but they prayed the 'sinner's prayer' with our Russian evangelists and received Christ right there on Jackson Square. God's Word is powerful in any language, amen?" Denny said, concluding testimony time.

Each year when I think, *God, it doesn't get any better than this,* more amazing stories come pouring in off the streets, some from the most unlikely places, and I get to be the scribe.

# A CHILD SHALL LEAD THEM

The Nissley-ettes go to Mardi Gras with their parents, and as they grow older, they, too, come back with amazing true stories. In 1998, twelve-year-old Melody found herself involved with a fortune teller.

"Come with me. You've got to meet her," Melody said.

"Meet who?" I asked.

"The fake astrologer. I told her all about you," Melody said,

"Wait a minute. First of all, what are you doing hanging out with astrologers, and second, what did you tell her about me?"

"I told her about the book you're writing. Come on, let's go. It's not what you think, just come on!" Melody grabbed my hand and dragged me away from where I was seated in the historic district known as Jackson Square.

I was there to observe and take notes. However, I was intrigued. I wanted to find out what Melody had gotten herself into. Even though it was Mardi Gras, I never expected Christ to show up in the person of a fortune teller wrapped in a faux leopard scarf.

Fake astrologist Gretchen's card table resembled the other dozen or so soothsayers whose tables were also designed to draw in unsuspecting tourists. A pile of colorful, oversized laminated cards covered the center of a painted tablecloth. Arrows pointing in every direction flowed out from an exciting focal point.

When Gretchen was between customers, I introduced myself.

"Hi. I'm Jodie, the writer Melody was telling you about. You must know I was a bit worried when Melody said she was friendly with a fortune teller."

Gretchen's looks were her hook. She appeared every bit enchanting as the others, so I asked, "Would you tell me what you're doing here?"

She told me how she counsels customers regarding their future, but instead of giving them a bunch of devilish hocus pocus, she enlightens them with the truth of God's Word.

"I see only two lines," she said, making a cross in my palm. "They both come to an end as will your life. And if you like, I'll tell you why these two lines cross and how it may affect your future."

She then demonstrated how she gently holds the customer's hand with both of hers and looks compellingly into their eyes.

"Do you know what these two lines mean? God is letting you know that His son Jesus died on a cross just like this one. Did you know that He did it because He loves you? Jesus loves you. The Bible tells us that God doesn't want us to seek out mediums or fortune tellers. The Bible warns us that they will defile us. The Lord wants you to know He is the Lord, your God, and He loves you enough to die for your sins."

Without letting go of my hand, Gretchen turned each brightly colored card over one at a time. A super condensed pictorial version of God's plan for redemption unfolded.

"See here? Jesus was born of a virgin. God sent His son to earth as a baby to be like one of us, He grew up and taught God's truth in the temple, but the religious crowd didn't accept Him. See here?"

She turned over another card. "He performed miracles and healed people. Jesus is the real hope of the world. He is the hope you're looking for, and your future is in His hands."

She thoughtfully revealed all the cards, which are then beautifully displayed, depicting the gospel message until the last card is unveiled—THERE IS ONE GOD. And then, with my hand (or the customer's hand) resting gently in her palm, she asked if she could pray. At the session's conclusion, the fake astrologer gives each customer a handout containing the Scripture verses to confirm her statements.

God had given this woman a very unique ministry. She knew God would hold her responsible for what took place at her card table, and for that reason, she made sure there were Christians surrounding her who were committed to pray as she ministered.

Gretchen came to Mardi Gras from Oklahoma and camped out in the devil's playground where lies are sold for five bucks a pop. She was there to make sure God's truth, the truth that sets people free, was not only available, but tangible.

I asked Melody, "How'd you know she was a fake?"

"Well, I asked her if she would read my palm."

"You what!" I was shocked to hear this coming from a Nissley-ette.

"Here. Take a look," she said as she unfurled the inside of her palm. In permanent marker, Melody had written JESUS LOVES YOU.

"I went to all the fortune tellers and asked them to read my palm."

Of course, she did. She's Denny and Sandy Nissley's daughter.


## SMALL, BUT MIGHTY

Melody's sister Deborah was a preteen in New Orleans in 1999 when she handed a gospel tract to a homeless man on a bench.

"Give it to someone else," he said. "I can't read."

"I'll read it to you. It's my dad's testimony It's called The Funnel."

He sat straight up. "Yeah, I guess. That'll be okay."

"My name's Deborah Nissley, what's yours?"

"Johnny," he said with a smile.

He looked pleased someone had paid him some attention. Johnny had somehow managed to get by living on and off the streets for most of his life.

"Thank you, little Debbie. Ya know what? You're the first person ever to talk to me about Jesus. Could you explain Him to me?" the forty-four-year-old asked sincerely.

"Sure, Johnny. My dad, you see, was a really bad man. He got into drugs and stuff he shouldn't have. The devil messed up his life, but God put it all back together. He got saved when he asked Jesus to forgive him of all his sins. Yup. And he had a really bad accident. The doctors were going to cut off his leg, but God healed him, and now he's a preacher."

"Little Debbie, do you think I could get saved like the man in the story?"

"Yes, sir. Would you like me to pray with you? All you have to do is ask Jesus to forgive you and He'll come live inside your heart."

Johnny repeated the 'sinner's prayer' with eleven-year-old little Debbie. After spending only fifteen minutes with Deborah, Johnny was nearly weeping.

Denny arranged to meet Johnny the next day. Johnny told Denny that his greatest desire was to get off the streets. He said he was willing to do whatever was necessary, so the CIA team brought him to the church for a shave, a haircut, and a bath. Afterward, Johnny hopped into the Nissley family van with seven other homeless men to go to His Place, a ministry home in Alabama for men founded by Rick Hagans and his wife Kim.

Johnny blessed Denny with his parting words. "Denny, I wanna learn how to read so I can learn about Jesus. Give little Debbie a hug for me. God bless you. God bless you all!"

By virtue of God's grace and the goodness of a little girl who wasn't afraid to share the good news of God's plan for salvation, a man's life was redeemed and restored.

Christian soul winners who go to Mardi Gras can and should expect God to show up and do amazing things. People who go to Mardi Gras in hopes of experiencing the ultimate street party should be told there's no comparison to the feasting that will take place at the banquet table of the Lamb of God. Someone needs to tell them how to get a seat at the table since what they're really looking for takes place in heaven.

Thankfully, prior to Lent, Johnny, and hundreds like him on the streets of New Orleans, were offered the opportunity to hear the gospel message and find Christ...in action.

# JAILBIRD FOR JESUS

This is America, right?

"Repent! Turn from your sins!

That's what people expect from a street preacher, which can arouse spirited resistance in an irreligious crowd. Unfortunately, this was the situation when Denny, while waiting for a Christmas parade to begin, was arrested for demonstrating without a permit in December of 1998. The charges were eventually dropped because of his willingness to fight for his first amendment rights in his hometown of Manassas, Virginia.

When people stand on public property to proclaim Jesus, or satan, for that matter, Denny is adamant that it is illegal for anyone in American to stop them. Preachers of the gospel shouldn't fear the competition, only the prevention of free speech. Denny's message to Christians audiences usually includes a reminder that believers should regularly exercise their right to proclaim the Good News.

. . .

*In his own words...*

The first time I was arrested for preaching the gospel in a public place was during our first year in ministry in Greeley, Colorado. Christ in Action took in a grand total of $6,500 in 1982, so when I called home to tell Sandy I needed five hundred of those dollars to make bail, I might as well have asked for fifty thousand.

"Honey," Sandy had it all figured out. "Why don't you just sing. They'll let you out."

I knew back then that it was my privilege as an American, and my responsibility as a Christian, to fight for my right to free speech. I was more than willing to make it an issue and inclined to make a federal case out of it. Consequently, I did end up in federal court some years later.

During Spring Break 1985, I worked with a youth group from a church in Lakeworth, Florida. A group of us were walking down one of Fort Lauderdale's side streets packed with bars, restaurants, and gift shops. Sandy was out in the crowd taking pictures and I was carrying the cross.

I found two college students standing in line waiting to go in one of the trendy bars on the strip. It was around nine o'clock at night and the two students seemed interested in talking with me, so I took the cross off my shoulder, propped it upright, and stood in line with them while we talked about Jesus.

Out of nowhere came a deep voice, "Hey, buddy. You've got to keep moving. You're not allowed to stay still. That's loitering."

"Oh, really? I asked the police officer. "Why can't I wait in line like the rest of the people?"

"Because I said you can't. Now move it on down the street," he said, pointing.

"Okay. I'll go," I said as I picked up the cross. "But I don't understand why it's okay for these people to loiter."

He screamed as loud as he could. "Because I told you to move it!"

He was a substantial 6'4", 240 pounds, enforcer of the law with an attitude, so I decided it would be best for me to leave. I hadn't taken three steps when another officer stepped right in front of me. "Take it beachside," he snapped.

"What?"

"Take it beachside," he repeated, pointing to the other side of the street. As he pointed, he swung his fist six or seven times, throwing upper cut punches to my stomach, knocking me off balance, and pushing me off the sidewalk.

I tried to keep my composure. With the cross still on my shoulder, I assured him I was going. "Why are you hitting me? I'm leaving. I'm going!"

I turned to walk across the street when, all of a sudden, the officer started flipping out, yelling to the crowd, "Stop him! He's under arrest. You're under arrest!"

The scene quickly got chaotic. Someone jumped me from behind and the cross fell to the ground. That someone had a professional choke hold on me, and with his forearms locked around my throat, he was trying to expose my neck by pushing under my chin. Luckily, I caught a glimpse out of the corner of my eye and saw it was the angry police officer trying to strangle me.

I kept my chin down, put my hands up, and said, "Okay, man. Take it easy. I'm leaving!"

Suddenly, he thrust his knee into my lower back to elongate my spine so I would raise my chin. His arm came in directly under my Adam's apple, and I went out like a light. I woke up on the hood of a police squad car.

While I was unconscious, they had ripped my arms behind my back so hard my shoulder ligaments tore. My larynx and trachea had been crushed, splitting open my voice box. As they put me in the police car, I turned and caught a glimpse of Sandy and the flash of her camera.

They shoved me toward the open door but miscalculated their aim and smacked my head into the side of the car. Then, someone said, "Oh, yeah. I forgot. Watch your head, Reverend."

I was taken to a holding station and left there for two and a half hours. At the time, my physical condition was pretty bad. My shoulder throbbed, the muscles in my back twitched in torturous spasms, my hands cramped up due to the lack of circulation, and when I asked if I could use the bathroom, they had a good time laughing at me. They told me I'd have to wet my pants.

I was somewhat relieved when I heard, "Nissley, let's go. You've moving to central lock-up."

My only prayer was that there would be a bathroom there, and thank God there was.

## ONE WORD BIBLE STUDY

Nearly two hours went by before they took the handcuffs off. My hands and arms fell to my side, limp and aching as the blood rushed back into them. My fellow jail mates were drunks and street people, except for one fellow who let it be known that he was a millionaire businessman. He had a foul mouth and was in for drunk and disorderly conduct.

"Well, Reverend, whatcha in for?" he asked.

"I'm in here for preaching Jesus to two college students in front of a bar."

He wandered off only to return after a short while to ask, "Reverend. What's the word for today?"

"The word for today is the same for every day. The Bible says the wages of sin is death, but the free gift of God is eternal life in Christ Jesus."

He slapped me so hard across my face, it stunned me. I quickly prayed, *Jesus, don't let me hurt this man.* He walked away and returned to ask, "What's the word now, Reverend?"

I shared with him the next part of the gospel story, chapter, and verse. He slapped me again leaving my face stinging. After a half an hour, he returned and we did an instant replay, but this time when he walked away, I grabbed him by the collar of his expensive suit.

"Tell ya what, mister. You seem to be interested in words, so we're going to do a little word study here tonight. The word grace comes to mind. You've experienced three times already this evening. Let me explain it to you, grace means having unmerited favor given even though you don't deserve it. God's grace allowed me to restrain myself three times tonight, but I'm deeply concerned you've reached your limit. You see, God's grace is far more sufficient than mine. If you hit me again, and I retaliate, I want you to know that God did not fail. I failed God. To make it simple, the next time you hit me, I might flush you down that toilet, and if that happens, don't blame God. Blame me."

He rolled his eyes.

"Do you understand this?"

"Yes, Reverend. I do."

He didn't bother me again with his vain attempts to dishonor God. In fact, he was rather courteous during our remaining time together. It was three o'clock in the morning when they finally let me out on bail.

## DO RIGHT, IT PAYS

Due to my injuries, my medical bills were substantial, so I contacted an attorney. He suggested we sue the city of Fort Lauderdale, the police officers personally, and the bar due to the fact that one officer was a paid employee of the bar at the time. It took four and a half years to go through the system, but justice prevailed as I told my attorney it would.

I relied on Romans, chapter 13, verse 3 that says…

> "For rulers hold no terror for those who do right, but for those who do wrong. Do you want to be free from fear of the one in authority? Then do what is right and he will **commend** you."

I had faith to believe I would be commended.

Sandy and I agreed to let God be in control throughout the entire ordeal, and He rewarded us by letting us see His hand at work in every aspect of the incident. Before the case was over and a verdict announced, all kinds of people acknowledged God's sovereignty, especially those who had witnessed the trial's eight days of scrutiny.

Because ours was a first amendment and freedom of religion case, we received media attention and extensive press coverage. Law students were assigned to the courtroom to study the arguments. Our case was major news—the city of Fort Lauderdale, police officers, and a bar getting sued by a street preacher for seven different violations of the law.

## GOD INTO THE COURTROOM

Before the trial began, the attorneys on both sides grilled potential jurors about their spiritual beliefs. I took detailed notes. Our jury ended up with two Jewish women, a couple of lukewarm Christians, one backslidden fellow, one man under the influence of a born again fiancée, one undecided, and so on.

The temptation to preach was overwhelming. I informed my attorney that at some time during the course of the trial, I wanted the opportunity to preach. He thought I was being too radical, but having looked at my notes from our jury selection, he and I both knew precisely what these individuals needed to hear. How could I not preach?

Of course, my opportunity was provided when I was asked to demonstrate for the record exactly what it was I do on the streets. I said, "I'd be happy to, but it might get a little loud, Your Honor."

"That's all right, Reverend. Just give us a sample of what you do," he said.

"Okay, then I might say something like…Ladies and gentlemen, there are people within the sound of my voice who may not know Yeshua is Jesus, the Messiah, the One sent from God. There are some who know about Jesus, the Messiah, but have stopped serving Him and have gone astray. There are others who say they know Jesus but it's all in their heads. The Bible calls such people lukewarm and says God will spit them out of His mouth. Some may not have decided whether they even believe there is a God."

I mentioned every single juror's life situation and closed with the salvation message using a judge's perspective. "God is the just judge who judges all men's hearts. He's holy and…"

It quickly became apparent the evidence in the case weighed heavily in our favor. Sandy had not only taken photos of the beating and false arrest, but a pastor from Fort Lauderdale just happened to be in front of the bar with his video camera. He captured the whole thing on film.

When the defense tried to discredit the amateur videographer/pastor as a witness, it came out that this man was not only a pillar in the community, but he had also served as Fort Lauderdale's police chaplain. His testimony revealed that the Fort Lauderdale police department hired him to provide videography instructions, which became a real problem as they tried their best to tarnish his reputation.

As we left the courtroom that day, the day before the verdict, the judge and my attorney held the door open for me as I removed the cross from the federal courthouse. "Hey, Your Honor," I said playfully. "Need any lumber?"

"Ah, no, Reverend. I think you've found a very appropriate use of that lumber. I think what you're doing is...ah..." he scratched his chin, searching for the proper word. "...is very **commendable**."

"Did you hear that?" I asked my attorney later.

"Hear what?"

"The judge commended me."

"Well, why am I not surprised?" he laughed.

We rejoiced, sensing victory was soon to be ours. Although a victory would be rightfully ours, we determined God would get all the glory, which is precisely what happened when the jury declared the defendants guilty of unlawful arrest, unlawful and excessive force, unreasonable conditions of restraint, assault and battery. We were awarded a generous financial settlement to cover my medical and legal expenses, and then some.

Aside from acquiring an appreciation for the Apostle Paul's trials and tribulations, being beat up for preaching the gospel was not a fun experience. Yet, when I look back and see what God did, despite the devil's attempt to silence this street preacher, I become more determined to fight the good fight of faith. I can be as stubborn as God wants me to be.

## NABBED FOR NOTHING

It was Saturday, the fifth of December 1998, when a few Manassas police officers felt it was their duty to save and protect citizens from a fully devoted evangelical family who had come to celebrate Jesus, the reason for the season. Denny brought his family and his cross to the Christmas parade as a reminder that after the manger, comes a cross.

*In his own words...*

Our oldest daughter Rachel used a small public address system carried by a friend to lead the crowd in the Yuletide choruses. Our daughter Deborah offered tracts to people waiting along the parade route. It was quite a shock when two police officers on bicycles asked us to stop singing.

"You'll have to stop doing what you're doing," the officer informed me,

"Who? Us?"

"Yeah, you. You can't do this."

"Why not?"

"You're demonstrating without a permit. You need to get a permit."

"Oh, I see. But officer, I do have permission to do this."

"Where is it? Can I see it?"

He asked, so I told him.

"It's in the Library of Congress. It's called the Constitution of the United States of America. I believe what I'm doing here is covered under freedom of speech."

"Ah, well, you still can't demonstrate without a permit."

"Well, I'm not protesting or demonstrating against anything," I explained.

"What do you think you're doing?" he asked.

"Proclaiming!"

Neither policeman looked thrilled at the thought of having to deal with this situation, which was attracting more attention than we could have hoped for on our own.

"Look, you've got to do what you've got to do, but today's not the day I'm going to stop exercising my right to freedom of speech or religion."

"But the law in Manassas say…"

"Listen. I mean no disrespect, sir, but I don't care what law Manassas came up with. Do you realize it's illegal for Manassas to have a law on the books that is unconstitutional? Manassas should not have laws that supersede the Constitution. And if you enforce it, you become a law breaker."

"I don't think…"

"Well, I have thought about this. If you go ahead and arrest me, I'm gonna show up in court to fight this. This isn't the first time I've done this. I've been doing this for twenty years. I've never been convicted, never lost a case, and every time it happened that the police arrested me, the arresting officer has always gotten in trouble. In this case, that would be you. I'm talking about you."

"Listen. I've written this ticket many times. They come to court. They pay their fine, and they don't come back. I've never lost one of these," he said confidently.

"Well, this is interesting. Apparently, there's coming a day one of us is going to have a first-time experience. If it's me, I gotta pay a fine. If it's you, who knows what price you'll pay. I just hope it doesn't cost you your job." With that, I signed the warrant and was legally charged with demonstrating without a permit.

## UNBELIEVERS RALLY BEHIND THE STREET PREACHER

I turned to address the crowd. "Is there anybody here willing to testify in court about what just happened here?"

Hands went up everywhere. The police officers looked at each other.

"Hey! Can I get picture of the preacher getting arrested?" someone shouted from the growing crowd.

"Sure," I said. "I think that would be just great."

While I collected names, addresses, and phone numbers, a guy came up to me and said, "Hell, I think you're great! Keep it up, man. Good work. Can I shake your hand? Man, I'm not believing this. A preacher arrested for singing Christmas carols at a Christmas parade!"

"Hey, preacher. Look this way!'

"Hold on," I shouted back. "Make sure you get the cross in the picture!"

"Oh, yeah, right. Get that cross where I can see it. Now hold it."

The police officer was determined. "You know, you could go downtown, get yourself a permit, and you'd be okay."

"Not today. Not in time for the parade. And why should I? I don't need one. That's like getting a permit to drive down the street. I'm already allowed to drive down the street."

"You need a permit."

"Are you saying that to walk down the street and call out to people, 'Hey! Good morning, folks. Have a great day!' that I need a permit to do that?"

"No, that's legal," he said.

"Oh, but if I say in the same exact manner and tone, 'Good morning, folks. God loves you. Nobody loves you like Jesus!' or 'Jesus is the reason for the season' then I'm illegal?"

"Yes, sir. That is where the problem comes in."

"So, it's not that I'm calling out to the crowd. It's what I'm saying that's a problem for you. My choice of words is what's causing you to arrest me. Sound like religious discrimination to me."

"You got to understand, what you're doing has the potential to be a nuisance."

"Well, sir." I knew what was going to come next. I couldn't resist. "Again, I mean no disrespect, but you got to understand something. Your sins are a nuisance to God and that's why Jesus was born. Merry Christmas!"

The confrontation was going pretty well, I thought, until they questioned me about the ages of my daughters.

"You know, Mr. Nissley, because you have these minors, these young children, engaged in this illegal activity, there's more we could add to the charges."

The notion I was contributing to the delinquency of minors was despicable. The implication that I could be construed as an unfit parent made my blood boil. Americans need to know how far their country has strayed from its godly heritage. I had to pinch myself and ask, *This is America, right?* A friend contacted the mayor of the city of Manassas. The letter came to the mayor's desk from Chicago when my friend Kreg caught wind of my arrest.

*Dear Mayor Gillum,*

*I understand congratulations are in order. On December 5, 1998, your police officers were finally able to arrest the infamous Dr. Denny Nissley. And what is most surprising to me is that you were able to get him for singing Christmas carols at a Christmas parade. Disturbing the peace, I'm guessing. Someone told me it was because he was missing a permit. Could this be correct? I've known Denny for roughly fifteen years, and I've heard him sing. Though his voice is not angelic, I don't think it merits arrest, however, there are a number of incidents you might be interested in:*

*In October of 1998, Denny loaded up his trucks with food and clothing and brought these much-needed supplies to the flood-ravished victims in Cuero, Texas. I understand he fed not only the people of Cuero, but he also fed the utility and Red Cross workers who were there to restore order to the devastated community. I'm not sure if he cooked the food or not, but in all likelihood, he most probably overlooked obtaining a permit. Also, I'm pretty sure the work he did to help put lives back together was not cleared through the union and may have violated someone's right to work.*

*Every year since I've known Denny Nissley he has spent time and energy organizing Christian outreach ministries to reach the people who wouldn't ordinarily go to religious services. He does this at great personal expense. I've seen perfectly good alcoholics and homeless people be transformed and changed by his message of hope and the tangible love he offers. Perhaps you could nab him on some sort of meddling charge.*

*When I found out you were onto this guy, I was relieved. Finally, someone in authority knows Denny has been bold enough to share the transforming power of his faith to people like his neighbor, an owner of a handful of porno shops in the Washington, DC area. God forbid this kind of a man becomes a good-hearted Christian and closes those wonderful places of business. I maintain Nissley must be stopped before his actions have a direct impact on the city's tax revenues.*

*I have many other stories to share with you about this street preacher, but I've probably already given you sufficient information about the character of this man and the nature of his agenda. Mr. Mayor, my sarcastic comments are intended to help clarify the foulness of arresting someone for singing Christmas carols at a Christmas parade. Might we agree that Denny's only oversight was bringing the wrong prop? Perhaps he should have carried a manger instead of a ten-foot cross.*

*Sincerely,*

*Kreg Yingst*

~

The charges stemming from Denny's arrest, which received national attention in both secular and Christian media outlets, were dismissed. The American Center for Law and Justice released a press statement on March 1, 1999, stating that although they could not speak for the Manassas City attorney, who did not specify his reasons for dismissing the case, they felt it was wise for the City attorney to reconsider his decision to prosecute people guilty of exercising their right to speak about their religious beliefs in a public forum.

And now, when one of the Nissley-ettes starts to sing in public, someone in the family calls out, "Hey! Be quiet! You'll get Daddy arrested!"

Needless to say, Denny maintains a close relationship with some of the best attorneys in America.

# LIFE WITH THE NISSLEYS

At one time, you could get a dozen road warriors for Jesus for the price of one evangelist. Because of Denny's steadfast determination not to let his ministry come between him and his growing family, the Nissleys traveled together as much as possible. Some years, they were on the road more than they were at home.

Vehicles and children increased over the years, which meant CIA maintained a fleet of vehicles that included their MCI motorcoach, a fifteen-passenger van, utility trucks and trailers for their mobile kitchen, and a Peterbuilt semi-truck with an extended cab and 48-foot trailer that housed a custom-built, mobile stage and gigantic outdoor tent, large enough to shelter up to 1,100 people.

The Nissley's faithfulness to the call of God on their lives can't be denied. I haven't met another family so unrestrained by the cares of this world and compelled by the love of Christ that they pursue God's call on a moment's notice, no matter where it takes them. If Denny weren't in ministry, I'm convinced he'd be a millionaire. If he were a salesman, he'd reach every goal and break every record. He's unstoppable. Thankfully, Denny is wholly devoted to a Person, not a business plan or line of products.

After being in ministry and on the road for Jesus for twelve years, Denny and Sandy wanted to experience a true family vacation, something they had cheerfully sacrificed since establishing the ministry. At the time, Denny admitted to being close to burn out.

After a ministry conference in Oregon, a ministry supporter gave Denny $5,000, designated for a recreational family vacation. At the same time, a businessman from Pennsylvania gave Denny his Texaco credit card with permission to fill the bus with fuel, which enabled them to take a well-deserved leave of absence. Clearly, the Lord wanted the Nissleys to take a break, so they did.

They were having the time of their lives on sabbatical, but vacation funds were getting low, as was the gauge on the gas tank. They were relaxing in Sturgis, South Dakota when Denny called the toll-free number on the back of the gas card to find the location of the nearest Texaco station. He received instructions and directions, including the exit number in Sundance, Wyoming.

He planned on telling his friend that his gas card would be used again in Wyoming. It was Saturday when he made the call.

"Hey, Denny!" his friend said. "Funny you should catch me. I'm usually not home on Saturday."

This was before everyone had a cell phone in their pocket.

"Yeah, I know. I got the gas card. Really appreciate it, man! We took off like you said."

"How's your cash holding up?"

"To be honest with you, we're pretty low at the moment. We're having a great time, but that also means we've been spending money."

"I'd like to get you some cash. Where are you?"

"I'm at the Texaco station in Sundance Wyoming. Out in the middle of nowhere."

"Denny. You're in a phone booth, right? Turn around and look across the street. What do you see?"

"Ah, well, I see a big house."

"Surrounded by a white picket fence? Is the house still that pinkish color?"

"Woah, how'd you know that?"

"Hang up and call me back in fifteen minutes."

Denny hung up, willing to trust his friend for fifteen minutes.

"Denny, do you have something to write with? Write this down," came the instructions. "This lady has $350 cash. She's going to give it to you in fifteen minutes. She wants to meet you and Sandy and the kids."

"Excuse me," Denny said. "What's happening?"

"I go antelope hunting in Wyoming every year and I stay at her house in Sundance. I get my fuel at that Texaco station where you're calling me from. I'm going to mail her a check for the money, and by the way, keep the gas card, brother!"

A coincidence? A fluke? Not a chance. These were not random events. It was God's plan to bless the Nissleys. They trusted God for a great vacation, and He gave it to them. But the story doesn't end there.

## SPLURGE

At the end of their vacation, on Mother's Day, they were in Spokane, Washington. The desire of Denny's heart was to splurge and give his wife Sandy two nights of luxurious rest at a fine hotel. He called ahead and booked adjoining rooms, complete with a hot tub, a fireplace, a king size bed for Denny and Sandy, and glow-in-the-dark stars on the ceiling for the kids' room. It was called splurging for a reason. It was out of the ordinary and it was going to cost more than they were used to paying for lodging.

Denny had arranged for their ministry office to forward their mail so they wouldn't be overwhelmed with unopened mail when they returned home. In the middle of the stack of mail was a personal letter from a fellow street preacher. A check for $500 fell out.

"Heard you and the family finally took a vacation. I wanted to give you this so you could splurge. God bless!"

The hotel bill and room charges came to exactly $502, which came to no surprise to this scribe. Serving God is the most thrill-filled, miraculous adventure anyone can have. No one can convince me otherwise. When you look back and see evidence of God's extraordinary and supernatural blessing, it's compelling. I get overwhelmed, dizzy with pure delight and gratitude when I realize how God takes care of His kids, in this case, the evangelists who take the love of Jesus where it's desperately needed and hardest to find.

I'm not an intellectual, but I understand the beginning of wisdom is to fear God. I don't have the gift of evangelism, or of healing, but I pray for lost and sick people. I am called to be a holy scribe for amazing true stories that exemplify God's unconditional love. I'm also called to cultivate hidden potential in marginalized communities. Currently, that means volunteering in a state prison for convicted male felons. You may not be called to be a prison volunteer, or a scribe, or a street preacher, but you can still be Christ...in action. The key is to remember to fear God, not evil.

To learn more about Christ in Action ministries, visit their website: www.christinaction.com

# EPILOGUE

**W**hy fear God?

Now that the part about not fearing evil has been thoroughly proven, it's time to methodically solve life's most important question. Why Christianity? Why fear the God of the Bible, in other words. I like to use the analogy found in The Evidence Bible called The Choice.

Imagine the excitement you would have if offered a choice of four gifts:

- The original Mona Lisa
- The keys to a brand new Lamborghini (or vehicle of your choice)
- A million dollars in cash
- A parachute

You can only pick one. Which one would you choose? Before you decide, you'll need some information that will help you make the wisest choice. *You have to jump 10,000 feet out of an airplane.*

That bit of information should help you resolve this issue of which gift to choose. The parachute is the only gift that will help you; all the others are useless. The revelation that you have to jump out of an airplane and face the law of gravity should produce a healthy fear in you, the kind of fear that is good because it can save your life.

Since all of humanity stands on the edge of eternity, let's compare the four major religion:

- Hinduism
- Buddhism
- Islam
- Christianity

Which one should you choose? Before you decide there is some information that will help you determine which one is the wisest choice. We're all going to die. No one gets out of this life alive. Is there a law, like the irrefutable law of gravity, that can help you decide which religion you should choose?

The answer is yes. It's called the law of sin and death. We know it as the Ten Commandments. These commandments reflect God's nature in that they contain the universal and unchanging principles of morality. Their purpose is to describe our relationship to God and our fellow human beings. The reason God cannot tolerate sin is that it a defilement of His character. Fortunately for us, His commandments lead to mercy and truth.

## GOD'S COMMANDMENTS IN A NUTSHELL

**You shall have no other gods before me.** Do you love Him with all of your heart, soul, mind, and strength? That's what the first commandment requires.

**Have you created a god in your mind** that makes you feel comfortable and less judged? That is idolatry. The second commandment says that is not allowed.

**Have you used God's name in vain,** as in as a cuss word to express disgust? That's called blasphemy, and it is not allowed and breaks the third commandment. **Have you honored your parents and kept the Sabbath holy?** If not, you've broken the fourth and fifth commandments. **Have you ever hated someone?** The Bible says anyone who hates his brother is a murderer. The seventh commandment says you shouldn't commit adultery, but the Bible tells us that anyone who **looks at a person with lust** commits adultery in their heart. **Have you ever lied? Every taken anything without paying for it? Have you ever jealously desired other people's things?**

These are the tenets of God's moral law that we will be judged by on Judgement Day when we stand before God to be declared innocent or guilty, which then results in a ticket to heaven or hell. Perhaps the idea of spending eternity in hell doesn't bother you. That's like saying you don't believe there will be any consequences if you jump out of an airplane without a parachute. Sinning against God comes naturally to us. We naturally earn His anger by our sins.

Many people believe that because God is good, He will forgive everyone and let sinners into heaven. If that is you, then you misunderstand God's goodness. The only way anyone can stand in the presence of God is to be pure in heart. This is an extremely fearful thought. The fear of God is the healthiest fear you can have.

Knowledge of God's law produces a fear that makes the news of Jesus Christ, a Savior, the wisest choice of all the religions. It solves the problem of God's wrath (His justifiable anger) because God's wrath was silenced at Calvary when *"Christ redeemed us from the curse of the law, having become a curse for us."* Galatians 3:13

We no longer need to fear death. We don't need to look any further for ways to deal with the dilemma of sin and God's wrath.

Let's go back to the four religions.

The religion of Hinduism says that if you've been bad, you may come back in another life as a lowly animal. If you've been good, you may come back as a more successful person. In other words, if you jump out of the airplane, you'll get sucked back so you can try again but this time as different passenger.

Amazingly, the religion of Buddhism denies that God exists. It teaches that life and death are an illusion. That's like standing at the open door of the airplane and saying, "I'm not really here, and there's no such thing as the law of gravity, and there's no ground to hit."

Islam acknowledges the reality of sin and the justice of God, but the hope it offers is that sinners can escape God's justice if they perform enough religious works. The hope is that God will see and offer mercy, but there's no way to be sure. Works will be judged on Judgement Day. It will be decided then based on whether Islam has been followed, repentance has been sincere, and enough righteous deeds were done to outweigh the bad ones. Islam teaches that you can earn God's mercy, in other words. That's like jumping out of the airplane and believing that enough flapping your arms will counter the law of gravity and save you from hitting the ground.

**So why is Christianity different and the best choice?**

Christianity is the best choice because God provided a parachute. God was in Christ and reconciled the world to Himself through the sacrificial death of His Son Jesus Christ. God loves us so much that He became a sinless human so He could satisfy the penalty contain in the law of sin and death. Only Jesus can save us from death and hell. The Bible is one long invitation to come to Jesus. In Him, you'll find the meaning and purpose of your life. Part of that purpose is to invite others to come, so that they too will find refreshment and fulfillment in the water of life that Jesus pours out on all who come to him.

Salvation is something we don't deserve, nor is it something we can earn it by doing good works. And since we can't know when we will jump through the door of death, it makes sense to put on the Lord Jesus Christ as you would a parachute. Trust Him, and only Him for salvation. Throw yourself on the mercy of the Judge. He is rich in mercy to all who call on Him.

> Seek the Lord while He may be found, call upon Him while He is near.
> Let the wicked forsake his way, and the unrighteous man his thoughts.
> Let him return to the Lord and He will have mercy on him, and to our
> God, for He will abundantly pardon. **Isaiah 55: 6-7**

The fear of God is truly the beginning of wisdom.

# ABOUT THE AUTHOR

Jodie Randisi established her author coaching and publishing business to help ordinary people with extraordinary true stories get published. COWCATCHER Publications specializes in inspirational memoirs and activity books as well as career-enhancing books for business owners. Jodie is a professional speaker. Her speaking topics are highlighted and promoted at womenspeakers.com. (**https://bit.ly/3zyPLdo**)

Randisi is also known for cultivating hidden potential in marginalized communities. She was awarded Outstanding Toastmaster of the Year in 2017 for the volunteer work she does coordinating Toastmaster prison clubs in South Carolina. She facilitates prison book clubs and teaches life coaching classes because she understands education is essential for rehabilitation. Jodie was a featured speaker at the TEDx Women event held on Hilton Head in 2018. Her presentation, *The Art and Science of Kindness*, can be viewed here: (**https://youtu.be/b-W6K4Ncp84**)

## FREE BONUS OFFER

You're invited to download YOUR STORY MATTERS, an 18-page PDF document featuring three strategies for sharing Christ: (**http://bit.ly/3KtNqqd**) It's about what to do when God wants to use you, not the evangelist. For anyone interested in learning more about scheduling a live (or virtual) YOUR STORY MATTERS workshop: (**https://calendly.com/coach-jodie/letschat**)

Made in United States
North Haven, CT
10 May 2023

36431476R00095